ALMOST
Close Still Counts With God

Thank you For TAKING
THE TIME TO READ my
Book. MAY ALL oF YouR
"ALMOST" moments GLoRIFY GoD!

Dale Presley

Dale Presley

1

To my lovely wife Laura - Thank you for your encouragement in the process of writing this book. Thank you for always being by my side. May the Lord give us both many more years of marriage together.

To Kaleb and Jakob- I love you both so dearly. You're both cherished gifts from God. You always make me a proud Dad.

To my Mother and Father- Thank you for your Godly upbringing. The Lord couldn't have put me into a more loving atmosphere than you both provided for me. Thank you for showing me what a Godly marriage is supposed to look like.

ACKNOWLEDGMENTS

So many people have contributed to this book, that it would be difficult to name them all. However, I would like to single out a few for my thanks.

Jessica Fischer, Joy Presley and Kendra Haines for taking the time to review and make corrections to my book. I couldn't have done it without any of you!

To my siblings, Mike, Brian, Mark & Milissa, for encouraging me to get the book out.

James Flamm, what a great friend and brother in Christ you are to me. I wouldn't have written this book without your encouragement to do so.

Wally & Dorris Robbins, thank you for your Godly example of marriage. Thank you for allowing me to put you into this book, so that others may marvel at what God can do for a couple throughout their lifetime together.

TABLE OF CONTENTS

Introduction and Background

I grew up in the big city of San Diego, CA. I was born into a loving, Christian family. Both of my parents are still married today, and have been an inspiration to me. I am the oldest of five kids. I have three brothers and one sister who is a fraternal twin to my youngest brother. From the time I was born my parents took me to church at Clairemont Emmanuel Baptist Church. I attended this church for the first thirty-three years of my life. I graduated from high school in 1988 and started attending college studying Administration of Justice, which I "Almost" finished. In 1989 I met my beautiful bride-to-be. My wife Laura and I were married on Dec 31, 1994. We have two wonderful boys, Kaleb, 13, and Jakob, 9. We now make our home in Chandler, AZ, since moving there in 1993. Our church family is Mesa Baptist Church, where I am active in the choir and Sunday school.

My inspiration for writing this book comes from the godly friends in my life. My belief is that everyone's life is made up of "Almost" moments. Each of us, day by day, struggle with different issues and sin. I have come to grips with the fact that as long as I live on this earth I will always have "Almost" moments. Due to sin in the world, and in each of us, we can never have perfection on earth. Romans 6:23 says, "For the wages of sin is death, but the gift of God is eternal life in Christ Jesus our Lord." Sin is going to keep us in the "Almost" status, but glory to God that in the second part of this verse there is a gift of eternal life in Christ Jesus for those who believe. John 3:16 states, "For God so loved the world that he gave his one and only Son, that whoever believes in him shall not perish but have eternal life." The only person that has ever lived to not have "Almost" events is Jesus Christ. He is the only one to have had no sin. I hope as you read this book you can find a little of yourself in these pages. Hold onto the truth that sometimes, close still counts with God!

Chapter 1 "Almost" Popular Growing Up

I was born into a loving, Christian home. The love of Christ was always taught and demonstrated in my house. I was a very hyperactive child growing up. Doctors really did not diagnose Attention Deficit Hyperactivity Disorder (ADHD) back then. I was just viewed as being an active boy. When you couple this with the "type A" personality that God gave me – whew! Watch out! My parents had their hands full with me. Thank God that he gave me patient parents. If I'd had any other parents, I may not be here today to write this book.

It was very difficult growing up as the oldest child. The expectations placed on me at times were pressure packed! I often heard, "You should know better, because you're the oldest." It was my job to set a good example for the younger ones. Discipline was always a part of my life. It still is today, only it takes a different form now. My father and mother always believed in the following verse,

Proverbs 13:24, "He who spares the rod hates his son, but he who loves him is careful to discipline him." Now at the time I was being spanked I sure was not feeling much love. However, my parents never disciplined me with anger, but with the love of Jesus. It was always explained to me why I was going to be disciplined. The words, "This will hurt me more than it hurts you," were often spoken. Being a parent now, I can see clearly that my parents were willing to selflessly hurt me a little then, so that I would not be hurt even worse later. This is demonstrated in Proverbs 3:12, "...because the Lord disciplines those he loves, as a father the son he delights in." I have come to understand that discipline done in a godly manner is the only way to show true love to your child.

~

I started kindergarten at age five. I should have known that I was doomed on my very first day of school. I was going to start my real education the hard way. Being ADHD and a "type A" personality is not a good combination. To top it off I was taught right from wrong, and I felt it was partly my job to make sure right prevailed at all cost. If right was not being done, then I was going to set it right. That meant I was the most dreaded of all kids in school, the "Tattle Teller." That's right! I was one of "those" kids in school. I just knew the teacher had only one set of eyes, and I felt it was my job to have her back. Well to this day I am not even sure what it was that I tattled on a certain kid about. I just remember the consequences of my actions. At lunch time, he took a lunch baggy filled with water, and popped it in front of my pants. This made it look as though I had an accident. The kids started laughing at me. The teacher

9

said, "It's alright, accidents happen." She sent me home to change. My parents said the same thing, "Accidents happen." I was trying to explain what happened, but no one would believe me. Well, I "Almost" made it through my first day of school without a hitch.

Either kids never understood me, or I just could not understand kids. I was always the teacher's pet. I even brought apples to school with me. Kids, if you are failing a grade, this actually helps bolster your grade in the class! No, do not actually bribe your teacher. I am kidding of course! I always found more wisdom in the people older than me. I wanted to always hang around adults and be a part of their conversations. I was always trying to grow up too fast. I see a lot of this happening in our society today. Parents, please encourage your kids to stay kids until they are actually adults. Being "Almost" popular with my teachers, or parents' friends is not always the way to go.

At the tender young age of eight, I heard the whisper of God's calling on my life. In the summertime my parents would host a week of the Good News Club in the front yard of our home. This was similar to a Vacation Bible School program. Elinor Cooper started these clubs, and I am eternally grateful for her faithfulness to Jesus. Jesus is still using her in mighty ways today to reach lost children. This is the first time in my life that I can recall having fully accepted Christ's death on the cross and resurrection. I had always heard about Christ, but had not come to an age of really understanding what it meant until then. There have been other times in my life when I have reaffirmed my faith in Jesus, but this was the main event. I knew at that point that I went from "Almost" saved to being secure in where I would spend eternity.

Trips with the family at a young age were fun, and scary. One thing that we always did before starting any trip was to pray that the Lord would put a hedge of protection around us, going and coming. It is still something I do with my family today. My parents had a gold Ford Pinto station wagon with back seats that folded down to make more room. One trip in particular that I have vivid memories of, is our trip from San Diego all the way to Arkansas. At that time there were just my parents and my two brothers, Mike and Brian. Each of the kids took turns in the passenger seat at four hour intervals, to help keep my mom or dad awake. The other three would squish together in the back and sleep. My parents did not have a lot of money, or a great amount of vacation time. Therefore, we did not make stops at hotels. Also, if we had to go to the bathroom before the prescribed four hour gas-ups, then we were out of luck. I made sure to save my drink cup! The night we came into town in Arkansas it was pouring cats and dogs. My grandparents lived in the country, five miles from the nearest paved road. When we turned off the paved road onto the small dirt road (which was now a soupy mud), it became very interesting. I had never seen pitch black like this before. The headlights barely lit the way through the hard rain. My dad suddenly stopped for no apparent reason. Then he got out of the car to assess the situation. Due to the rain, the creek (which was usually pretty dry) was a raging river. We could not phone AAA to help us out and my dad needed help. So I got out and helped pile up rocks in the raging river. Once we had built up enough rocks we got back into the car. My dad then said another prayer because he was not quite sure if the rocks would hold. He slowly moved the car across, and we made it to the other side. That was the night that a Ford Pinto "Almost" turned into Noah's Ark!

Growing up in a house with boys had its tense moments, especially when it came to my next oldest brother, Mike, who is only eighteen months younger than me. He just always knew how to push my buttons and took extra special delight in seeing how far he could push me before I would lose my temper. It is not a good idea to make an ADHD "type A" personality person angry. Growing up I had a horrible temper. One day my brother and I got into a knock-down, drag out fight. On this day my brother was getting the better of me and I just could not let that happen. I went and grabbed a knife and began to chase him. That was not a smart move, but I was not thinking clearly at that time. My brother ran into the bathroom and locked the door. I proceeded to put my fist through the door to try to get to him. Luckily, my parents came to save the day. Boy the discipline was sure harsh on that day! This was the day I "Almost" killed my brother. Now my brother and I love each other. Thank God I was not able to get to him that day!

~

Fraternal twins! In January of 1981, my mother gave birth to twins. Now up until this point there were already three boys. My parents were only trying for one more to get a girl, so twins turned out to be a big surprise. I remember being at soccer practice where my dad was the coach. My mother drove to the practice and walked across a whole soccer field to tell my dad she had something important to tell him. Then she simply turned around and walked back to her car. Well, my dad called practice early that day. When my parents told me the news, my first reaction was, don't we have enough already? Being the oldest of two others was hard enough, but now I was going to be the oldest of four other children, two of them being babies. My parents never wanted to know what the sex of the twins were. On the day of their birth, the doctor told my parents that the babies' heart rates were the same. He stated that whatever the first child's sex was, that the second would be the same. The first one born was my brother, Mark. My mother said, "Just put him back, I wanted a girl!" Then, a little more than five grueling minutes later, my only sister Milissa, was born. The screams of joy from my mom were over powering. I think people must have thought she hit the lottery! That day, my mom came very close to "Almost" having all boys. Thank God he gave her a girl, or I would have probably been the oldest of twenty by now. Whew, that was a close one!

At the age of twelve I was in the sixth grade and did not have any friends. As a matter of fact, I was beaten up quite often on the way home from school, usually by the same four bullies. They picked me up and threw me over a fence. They hit me and called me names. All of this was very hurtful. It did not help that as a young Christian I would take Biblical scripture out of context. Specifically, Luke 6:29, "If someone slaps you on one cheek, turn to him the other also." I would actually quote that scripture as I was being beaten up. I would actually turn the other cheek, and let them strike me on the other side. At this moment you are probably laughing. Well, so am I, as I recall those memories and write them onto paper. Somehow I felt that by showing the other cheek and literally telling them to hit me again, that I would win these kids over to Christ and they would be my friends. This is another "Almost" popular moment that did not turn out very well.

Be careful what you pray for at any age! This same year, in the sixth grade, I was so lonely and need of a friend. This notion crossed my mind that if I had some of the attributes of the popular kids, then maybe I in turn would be popular as well. I noticed that the popular kids all wore glasses. Well I knew that God answers prayers, so I began to fervently pray that my eyes would go bad. About two months later I was experiencing horrific headaches while reading. The teacher suggested that my parents take me to the eye doctor and, guess what! I now needed glasses to read! I was elated – overwhelmed with utter joy! Finally, I was going to be among the popular, the "in" crowd. I was shocked to find out that I was only ridiculed even more than before I had glasses. This was a point where I believe God had a sense of humor. God uses this sense of humor to get teachable applications through to us. He answered my prayer in a way that did not hurt me, but in the end opened my eyes even more clearly. About two weeks later, at church, the pastor was speaking on Ephesians, Chapter 1. When he read verse 18, I knew that God was speaking right at me like a parable, explaining how to see. The verse states, "I pray also that the eyes of your heart may be enlightened in order that you may know the hope to which he has called you, the riches of his glorious inheritance…" He was saying, "Hey, Dale! I want you to see with your heart first, not your eyes!" We so often miss God's message by twelve inches, from our head to our heart. The glasses prayer is another example of "Almost" being popular.

This story also causes me to think about what Jesus was doing when he was only twelve years old. We see a snapshot of his life at this age in Luke 2:41-49:

> 41 Every year Jesus' parents went to Jerusalem for the Festival of the Passover. 42 When he was twelve years old, they went up to the festival, according to the custom. 43 After the festival was over, while his parents were returning home, the boy Jesus stayed behind in Jerusalem, but they were unaware of it. 44 Thinking he was in their company, they traveled on for a day. Then they began looking for him among their relatives and friends. 45 When they did not find him, they went back to Jerusalem to look for him. 46 After three days they found him in the temple courts, sitting among the teachers, listening to them and asking them questions. 47 Everyone who heard him was amazed at his understanding and his answers. 48 When his parents saw him, they were astonished. His mother said to him, "Son, why have you treated us like this? Your father and I have been anxiously searching for you." 49 "Why were you searching for me?" he asked. "Didn't you know I had to be in my Father's house?"

This story gives us an amazing glimpse of the life of Jesus when he was twelve years old. It makes you think of a few things. For one, how did his parents not notice him missing for a complete day? If that happened today, I am quite sure the parents would be brought up on neglect charges.

Second, it took them three days to finally find him, because he was in the temple courts soaking everything in. Finally, when he was found, he was not worried at all. Believe me, if I were separated from my mother and father at age twelve for five minutes, I would have been panicking! But it did not bother Jesus. You see his parents scolding him by saying, "Why have you treated us like this?" If this had been you or I in this situation we would have had a lot of explaining to do. Not Jesus! He had to be about his Father's business. He was never really alone. The Father in Heaven was there with him the whole time. If I could have only grasped the concept that being "Almost" popular was not as important as my proximity to the Heavenly Father, it would have saved me from a lot of other "Almost" moments.

~

I believe I was either twelve or thirteen when I was coming back from church camp on a bus. Everywhere I had tried to sit, I was pushed aside. Not a single kid wanted to sit by me. The youth pastor forced me to sit next to a girl that is still a great friend today, Karin. Now Karin did not want to sit next to me either at first. About half way home, we stopped at a McDonald's to get lunch. To say thank you for allowing me to sit next to her, I bought her a Miss Piggy glass. I also got one for myself, and still have it to this day. We became close friends. Well one day after playing at my house, we got on our bikes and rode to her house. Before we went around the final corner to her house I stopped. I was about to embark on a rite of passage at that moment. I politely asked her if I may give her a kiss. She said, "Of course you can." So we both extended our heads and necks out as far as they would go, making sure that four other people could have fit in the distance between the two of us. Then the "Almost" kiss took place. I call it that, because the amount of time my lips were connected with hers was barely more than a nanosecond. It was the classic touch and go. Our young love unfortunately did not last too long. Peer pressure from other girls at school made it too uncomfortable for her to be seen with me. It is still amazing though that through it all God has allowed us to remain such great friends over the years. I bet you are laughing again at my "Almost" first kiss. What a great memory to hold onto, and I hope you remember yours as well.

~

Those first few years as a teen I struggled with who I was, and puberty was very tough. It was especially difficult when I was fourteen and fifteen years old. When you throw a kid who is trying to become a man into the frying pan of life, during a time when he has no friends, it spells "Almost" disaster! At that age every teenager is trying to find their own way. None of them really understands how hurtful their words are. At this age I thought that this was the world, and nothing was beyond this. I just could not see past my teenage years. My heart ached, and tears often flowed down my face. All of me just longed to be loved and accepted. I firmly believe that the puberty phase of life is when we are the most fragile. Due to this being such a fragile time, I want to encourage those of you who are parents to be very in tune with your child. If they seem withdrawn, or speak of harming themselves, take it seriously!

Remembering that time in my life is bringing tears to my eyes as I write this. My favorite Christian band at the time was Petra. One of the songs they sang is called, "Annie," a song about a girl grabbing a bottle of pills and taking her own life. At the end of the song the lyrics say, "It's too late for Annie, she is gone for good. But it's not too late for you." All I heard when I listened to that song, was that it was time for me to kill myself. I "Almost" decided to commit suicide. I am not going to enlighten you on the plans I had to end my life, because that is not important now. The point is that even Christians struggle with taking their own lives, so always be vigilant in your love for others. That love could come at just the right time to save a person's life. I believe what finally pulled me out of my thoughts of deep despair was a very loving youth pastor named Eddie Passmore. Eddie was always so easy to talk to, he was never judgmental on any issue, and he always showed the love of Christ to all of the youth. He pointed me to a big time verse, Jeremiah 29:11, "'For I know the plans I have for you,' declares the Lord, 'plans to prosper you and not to harm you, plans to give you hope and a future.'" How could I possibly take my life after reading this verse? God had big, audacious plans for my life. He did not want harm to come to me. It was the lies of the world telling me these things. God then said he has plans for me in the future. That is just so big - I hope you can grasp it. If a person takes their own life, they are stopping God's future plans! God will always accomplish his mission, but he wants you in it until he has completed his work.

What is so sweet about being sixteen? For about a half a

year before turning sixteen I had my learners permit to drive. Boy, what an exciting time for me – and I bet a scary, nightmarish time for my parents. My dad would take me out to an empty Kmart parking lot late at night to practice my driving. The only things in danger were the light poles, some of which I think God had to pick up and put back down again. I really do not know how I missed some of them. Miracles can happen when your eyes are closed!

I was learning to drive in a 1976 Ford Van. This vehicle was a "three on the tree" column shifting with a clutch. Let me briefly explain, as some of you reading this may not know what a clutch is, let alone what "three on the tree" means. The vehicle shifter was on the right side of the steering wheel. Gear #1 is all the way forward and down. Gear #2 is slightly up then it slides back a little and up again. Gear #3 is straight down. Reverse was straight up from the Gear #1 position. So learning how to release the clutch with the right amount of gas, and trying to shift this van was not easy. Driving has become so simplified since then, that I'm sure had I been born in the 90's, I'd have had it made. The day finally arrived for my driving test at the Department of Motor Vehicles. I was so terrified to have this much older person whom I did not know hop into the passenger seat. He had half glasses that he would look over with his hard cold eyes. He had a clip board that he was writing away on, and I knew it was not good. When the test was over, my result was that I "Almost" got my license. Yep, I failed the driving test the first time around. What happened? I was so prepared! I blamed it on the vehicle, and that is my excuse that I stick with to this day. (I usually tell people out of embarrassment that I passed my driver's test the first time, through.) The DMV told me I had to wait another two weeks before I could retest.

Those two weeks were two of the longest weeks of my life. I already had a car that I bought with my own money - if you want to call it a car. It was a 1962 Ford Galaxie 500 that had more bondo on it than actual paint. It only cost me $250 – what a steal! I had already told everyone that I would have my license on that day. I was convinced that if I only had a driver license, I would be popular. Two weeks later I took the driving test again, but this time I borrowed an automatic. So I had my driver license - another rite of passage. Now I would be popular for sure! I thought everyone would want to ride with me. Sadly, having a license to drive did not make me more popular. It just meant that I had to spend a lot more money. I had to pay my own car insurance, which back in 1986 was $180 a month. That was almost the cost of my car! Also, on a good day it would get six miles per gallon. So, a car "Almost" made me popular.

In my junior year of high school I met my best friend, Dan Kendall. He had just moved to the San Diego area. This was a good thing for me, because he did not know yet that he was supposed to not like me. He showed up in one of my classes in the middle of the semester. I introduced myself, and he told me where he lived. His place was only two blocks away. That same night I went to his house, and knocked on his door. A look of shock was on his face that I was at his door. I am sure what was going through his head was, this guy who I just met a few hours ago is a stalker! Why did I tell a stalker my address? My need for a friend was so great that I became like a leach attaching myself to him. My overbearing demand for friendship "Almost" terminated this one before it started. I thank God for preparing Dan in advance for being able to be the friend I needed. The Lord had to have given him a lot of "Almost" moments as well to have the patience he had with me.

When I think of my friend, a few verses come to mind. Proverbs 18:24, "A man of many companions may come to ruin, but there is a friend who sticks closer than a brother," and Proverbs 17:17, "A friend loves at all times, and a brother is born for adversity." It took 17 years of my life before the Lord answered my prayers for a close friend. If you feel lonely, keep praying. Somewhere God is preparing the heart of just the right person to enter your life at just the right time. Hang onto that truth spoken in Deuteronomy 31:6, "Be strong and courageous. Do not be afraid or terrified because of them, for the Lord your God goes with you; he will never leave you nor forsake you."

~

Remember the 1962 Ford Galaxie 500 that I purchased for $250? This car "Almost" got me killed several times. On one occasion the road was wet from a recent rain storm. I was traveling east on the 8 freeway in San Diego, transitioning onto the 15 freeway going north. I was on the circular clover leaf to enter the freeway and just as I was about to merge from the turn, I hit the gas just a little. Well, a little was all it took with my car that weighed more than an army tank. I started to spin in circles across all five lanes of traffic. I came to a stop about a foot away from the center divider, and was now facing the oncoming traffic.

The whole thing happened in "God-mo," instead of slow-mo. I coined that phrase, God-mo because as I was spinning in circles I just knew for sure that an oncoming vehicle would strike me. Time in God-mo slows way down. This allowed God to send down hundreds of angels to take control of all of the other vehicles so that they would miss me. The other God-mo moment in my car was when I was headed down Genesee Avenue in San Diego, which has a rather large, steep hill. The passenger in my car – well, you guessed it I'm sure, Dan Kendall. As I started to go down the hill my accelerator stuck to the floor board. I was speeding up very quickly, and the light at the bottom of the hill was red! Dan was telling me, "Hey, Dale this isn't funny...put on the brakes! STOPPPPPPP!!!!" I tried to explain to him that I couldn't, and to brace for a terrible crash. My friend would have been very prepared had we crashed. His feet were on the dash board, and his head was between his knees, as he was literally ready to kiss his butt goodbye! At the very last moment God allowed the accelerator to become unstuck. I slammed on the brakes and stopped about one inch from a VW Bug. Whew! I would have squished this VW like a bug if I hadn't been able to stop. It's all very hilarious now looking back at it, but at the time that both of these were happening, I saw my life flash before my eyes. These moments convince me that while we should never test God, we can have peace knowing that if it's not our time to meet our Maker, He will provide a way out of the trouble. How do I know this? Well, in Psalms 46:1, it says, "God is our strength, an ever present help in trouble." Nice to know that in my "Almost" accidents, God is with me.

To summarize this chapter, God was in control and with me

the whole time I was "Almost" popular. Even though I kept seeking to be popular, that was not where the Lord wanted me. When I think back now, the kids that had it the roughest were the ones that were popular. They were invited to all of the parties. They were your jocks and cheerleaders. I'm not trying to say that none of the popular kids were right with God. I'm merely making a general statement that the Lord knew exactly what He was doing. The Lord was protecting my heart and mind from the negative situations that popular people can be placed in. By "Almost" being popular I was not invited to any parties or people's houses. I was not popular with the girls. You see by "Almost" being popular the Lord was actually keeping me from temptation. He knew that I wouldn't be able to resist the things of this world, so he put a bubble around me. I never had to deal with the temptation of taking drugs or smoking. I was one of the few kids I know that graduated high school still a virgin. Even as an adult I have had my struggles with wanting to be popular and noticed. I believe in order to truly be a Christ follower, you must first be willing to die to yourself. You must lay it all at the foot of the cross. Then you must take up the cross, and follow Jesus. The heart must be in a humble state to do these things. Popularity can lead to pride, which can get in your way of having a fulfilling life-long love relationship with the One that created you. Thank you, Jesus, for making me "Almost" popular growing up.

Chapter 2 "Almost" got my dream job.

Before diving into this section I would like to ask you a few thought provoking questions. Was there ever a time in your life when you fell short of your expectations? Did you work for something diligently only to come a fraction of a step away from it? Maybe you were in line for a promotion at work and someone who clearly didn't work as hard got the job? Maybe you're saying to yourself, "why can't I keep up with the Jones'?" "This person has more than I do!" "I went to school longer, so I should be entitled." Perhaps you have your dream job already. If so, congratulations – you don't have to read this chapter! Just kidding, of course. You shouldn't skip this section because you will get something out of it. I'm quite certain that if you have lived and worked any length of time in this world you have encountered one of the "Almost" moments I have just listed.

Well if you're even a little like me you have shook your fist at God in anger. God what do you want me to do with my life? Lord you say you love me, so what plans do you have for me? What is God's expectation in our lives as it relates to our work? In a moment I'm going to take you through a cursory look at my work history. I'm not doing this to brush up on my resume. I'm sincerely hoping that through my huge "Almost" dreams you will see that God has woven it all together for his purpose.

Lets first explore a little of what God says about work. We need to study this, so a right perspective can be derived. Right off the bat in Genesis 3:17, God spoke to Adam about work. To Adam he said, "Because you listened to your wife and ate from the tree about which I commanded you, You must not eat of it. Cursed is the ground because of you; through painful toil you will eat of it all the days of your life." This verse is pretty harsh! Let me tell you what the verse isn't implying first. Some people believe that work itself is cursed because of Adam. God doesn't say that working is cursed. He states that the ground is cursed. So the verse is saying that work is going to be really hard from now on. However, in the fruits of our labor we can still find joy. The byproduct of work is still good. An example of this principle is as follows: A woman has labor pains when working to deliver a child. Now according to my wife, the labor pains are horrible. This is a "thank God I'm a man" moment. Alright, back to the thought. The product of the work when it's finished is a beautiful baby. Nothing is more precious in life than the creation of life given by God. So remember, work is hard, but not bad. It's a necessary event to bask in the glory of what God intends to do with the process.

A few more verses tell us what our attitude should be towards work. Exodus 23:12 says, "Six days do your work, but on the seventh day do not work." Hey, what a great God! He is giving us a day of rest. He knows we will need to charge up our batteries again! 2 Thessalonians 3:10 states, "For even when we were with you, we gave you this rule, if a man will not work, he shall not eat." I believe God defines work in a lot of ways. If you're out of employment, but are actively looking for work, well that's your job at the time. If you're a couch potato expecting handouts from others, then this verse is referring to you. One last verse, which is one of my favorites is Colossians

3:23. It says, "Whatever you do, work at it with all of your heart, as working for the Lord." This is a verse that really sums up the word "Almost" got my dream job. You see, the verse doesn't say you get the prize. It simply tells us to give it our all, and let the Lord work out the rest.

Now I'm going to take you on my job journey. At the age of 10 I already knew what I wanted to do when I grew up. That's weird, I know. I haven't met too many people that had a definitive path they wanted to take so early in life. So at this young age, I just knew when I grew up that I would be a police officer. Of course, if your parents are anything like mine you may have heard, "Son/daughter, you can do anything you put your mind to!" Just a comment on that, if I may: Motivate your child to strive hard at everything. Do it for the Lord, and then even if it doesn't happen they will still be blessed. Telling your child he can be anything is a lie, because the sinful nature of men has some say in this area. As a child I asked my parents what they thought I needed to do in order to get my dream occupation. Good advice came my way. They said, "Work hard; don't steal; don't do drugs; and don't ever get in trouble with the law." Well, I can do all of those things, I thought. I'm on my way to my goal.

My first job at age 10 was to deliver the "Sentinel" newspaper in San Diego, CA. The manager would drop off the papers to me at my house. This paper was only delivered on Wednesdays and Saturdays. This job gave me a way to start working hard and building up responsibility. By the time I reached the age of 12 I was a pro at papers. It was time to move up a little. I started to work for the "San Diego Union" morning newspaper. This was a big jump at my age. The delivery demands went from two days a week to EVERYDAY – yikes! Not only that, the time of delivery was no longer in the afternoon when I got home from school. Now I was required to get up by three o'clock in the morning. When I started this job my route was about 50 papers. Within three years I built the route up to over 300 customers. The San Diego Union had a lot of contests for signing up new customers. I believe I won most of the contests. One of the ways I built up my customer base was to ask a potential customer if I could deliver the paper to them free for one week. Now this wasn't free at all. I paid for the extra copy, and made sure the paper was on their porch. Oh yeah, this was back when the paperboy had to put your paper on the porch, not the driveway. Wouldn't it be nice to go back to those days? The customer in most cases liked the paper, and liked my service. They would sign up with me, and almost never stopped taking it. The only day of the week that was hard to deliver was the Sunday paper. The Sunday paper is a brick designed to break potted flowers, and screen doors. My father would get up every Sunday and help me with this paper. He would put the extra papers in the van and meet me at different drop-off points. Then, as he was singing in the choir later that morning, I would watch as he desperately tried to stay awake! I appreciate my dad for showing such love by helping me during this period. Let me just take a small break from this dialogue. If you can think of a way that your parents impacted your life and it's possible to contact them, I encourage you to call and thank them! Alright, back to the journey. I did this job for eight years, only taking days off if I could find a substitute, and could afford to pay them. On several occasions I was sick as a dog, and I still had to do the job. I believe this taught me at an early age that I was being counted on, and couldn't let others down. If I didn't do it then the paper wouldn't be delivered. Learning that valuable lesson about responsibility still helps me today. For example, when an employer hires me to do a job, I know that if I'm not there, I'm letting the company down. It's important that children learn that it's not only themselves that are being let down when they don't show up for a commitment. Did I mention that there were a lot of skunks on my paper route? I can't even count the amount of times I "Almost" got sprayed!

This next entry is not exactly a job, but I will explain why it's in this section of the book. While in the eighth grade, some high school students from J.R.O.T.C. had an assembly at my school. J.R.O.T.C. stands for Junior Reserve Officers Training Corp. Up until this point my goal was to go out for junior varsity baseball the following year. I had been playing baseball from the time I was age five. My plans shifted drastically after seeing their demonstration. I listened to their recruiting pitch. So, I was "Almost" a jock in high school. The instructor told us how we would learn discipline. We would master all forms of drill. Drill is best defined as the moments we made while marching, or while handling a rifle. Speaking of rifles, boy was I excited to hear that I could learn to shoot. After the assembly I had more questions for the instructor. My aspirations to be a police officer were discussed. He immediately said that J.R.O.T.C was perfect for what my career goals were. He said, "A police organization is paramilitary in nature with its structure, and ranking system." He assured me that if I spent four years of high school in this program, I would be a hot commodity to get my dream job. So my mind was made up. I started

J.R.O.T.C the following year in high school. Some of the principles I came to learn early on are unfortunately still very prevalent in society today. For example, earning rank didn't have to do with how hard one worked. Moreover, it didn't matter how smart one was, or how many extra-curricular activities you were involved in. Instead, the whole system simply revolved around whether you were liked or not! With the end goal in mind, I tirelessly pressed forward. By the time my senior year came along I was just "Almost" an officer. Midway through that year, the person on staff as the S-4 didn't want to be on staff any longer. This position on staff was the lowest ranking officer position. You see, the S-4 was in charge of cleaning and fixing the damaged rifles that were broken during drill. It was the grunt position, but to make Officer, I stated I would gladly do it. Looking back, I still believe that the decision to choose J.R.O.T.C over baseball was the correct one. For even though it only "Almost" helped me get my dream job, it taught me so much more. For example, I was taught how to properly handle myself in a job interview. I also learned that maintaining eye contact with whom you are speaking is imperative! I also came to believe that being subordinate to someone in authority, even though you don't agree with them is something that should be taught to everyone. Of course, there was the spit shinning of shoes and ironing military creases that I could have done without! God knew what he was doing with me from the start. The Lord always sees the bigger picture.. My ability to speak boldly to anyone about the saving grace of Jesus is attributed to the leadership skills I acquired. The training I received those four years weren't wasted in my "Almost" getting my dream job. They were preparing me to glorify God in all things later in life.

Well it came time for me to want to drive and have a car. My parents always took care of the needs in my life, but when it came to my wants on the other hand, it was up to me! At the age of 16, and while still doing the paper route, I applied for another job. McDonald's hired me on the spot. The store manager said he had never before seen a 16 year old come to an interview wearing a suit and tie. He "Almost" started laughing hysterically at the sight of me. My hours were generally 5PM to 9PM, Monday through Friday, and 9AM to 5PM on Saturday. My only request when I started was that I not be scheduled on Sundays. I ended up later having to work a few Sundays but by and large, I was able to keep this day free for worshipping God. I honestly don't know how I made it through high school under this strenuous work load. If I was able to get four hours of sleep at night it was a miracle. It had to be the Lord taking my tests for me, because I couldn't have been awake! Here's a plug for McDonald's – kids these days look down upon having to work at a fast food establishment. I'm telling you that some of the most well adjusted, hard working people I know worked at McDonald's as a teenager. Their MDP, which stands for Management Development Program, is put together very well. By the time I turned 18 years of age I was promoted to management. Their training taught me that the customer is always right and to treat the customer how I would want to be treated. Some of their teaching had Godly principles in it. The second part of Matthew 19:19 states, "…and love your neighbor as yourself." Many times I had to interact with customers that were very upset with the product or service they received. In the back of my mind I kept saying, what would Jesus do? How would Jesus respond to this person? Can my attitude towards them reflect Christ? Can they just get a glimpse of the joy I have in my life? Never once did I lose my temper with a customer, and it's only God's peace in my life that made that possible. Also, every time a customer was upset I would ask myself how a police officer would handle the situation. Surely a law enforcement agency would want someone that can de-escalate a situation. I was sure at that moment in time that God was giving me the skills and moving me closer to "Almost" getting my dream job. Well, what did I really learn from all of this? I can cook a little. It doesn't bother me to clean up a nasty, flooded bathroom. I used to love shining up the brass poles. So many people would touch the brass throughout the day and leave their fingerprints all over those poles. You see so many people in our lives put their fingerprints all over us as well. We start to look very dull to others. God can come along in our lives and polish us up so we can shine for him and be ready to take on tomorrow's fingerprints. I bet you never thought God would use fast food to teach life lessons! Before I continue I just want to pause a moment to ask you another question. You have seen some of the things God has shown me in just a few of my jobs so far. Stop and think of what lessons have you learned from God in the places you have worked. I'm sure that if you write these things down on paper you will be praising God for giving you the jobs you had!

At the age of 19 I was enrolled at Miramar Community College. My major was Administration of Justice. Shortly after starting my classes I was hired on at University Towne Center in La Jolla, CA as a Mall Security Officer. Things were falling into place rather nicely. I was still on the path to "Almost" get my dream job. Being a Security

Officer at a big mall gave me a lot of experience dealing with different situations, and it seemed as though it was the perfect job to keep me moving toward reaching my goals. For example, this job had a rank structure similar to that of a law enforcement job. It was also mandatory to memorize radio codes for the job. These codes were the same as the police agencies used. Reports had to be written for anything that occurred, and a daily log also had to be filled out and turned in to the Sergeant for every shift. Furthermore, this job gave me the opportunity to meet and work with law enforcement officers "Almost" everyday! One day while I was in a patrol vehicle in the parking lot, I witnessed a big event. A white van pulled up to the stop light. All of the sudden, a women got out and ran away from her vehicle. I can't remember today if the van exploded or caught fire. At first the local police were involved. Then federal law enforcement started to show up. As it turned out, this was being investigated as a terrorist act against a famous navy captain's wife. This family lived close to the mall, so a stakeout was set up in order to watch over their home. A big mobile home was parked on our property for a little over a week. This was all very exciting, because the stakeout was being done by NCIS agents. On several occasions I would stop by and pester the agents. One of them was very kind to me and encouraged me to follow my dreams. This fueled my aspirations even more. This was the first of many security jobs that I took in order to stay close to law enforcement, so that I could "Almost" get my dream job.

When I was 20½ years old I hit the jackpot. It was such a happy moment in my life. After much preparation to get to this point I was hired onto the Mesa Police Department in

Mesa, AZ as a Police Recruit. Even better, the Lieutenant that hired me was a Christian man. He believed in me even at this young age. So off to Mesa, AZ I moved, so that I could start living the dream. Before the actual academy was to start, it was required of all of the recruits to go through a three week pre-academy. This was physically grueling to say the least. Unfortunately a sergeant in charge of this pre-academy didn't believe that I was old enough to be there, although up to this point the lieutenant had backed me up. Unfortunately, the lieutenant had a heart attack about a week and a half into the pre-academy. This allowed the sergeant to have free reign. About two weeks into the pre-academy, I became very ill. When I went to the doctor I was told that my temperature was at 104 degrees, and that I was not to return to work for at least one day. A doctor wrote me an excuse to be off from duty. When I returned, I was told that no matter what, missing a day of the pre-academy meant a loss of my job. This was a moment when I wept immensely! A lot of hurt flooded into my life as I recalled everything I had done to prepare for this. For a little while after that I went to work delivering chicken at Kentucky Fried Chicken. One of the regular customers would ask me what my aspirations in life were. As it turned out, this customer knew the Chief of Police for Mesa, AZ. She spoke with him about my situation. He ended up calling me and asked for my doctor's excuse. He said he would give me another shot, and I was hired back on to the department. I made sure that I was in much better physical shape going into the pre-academy this time around. However, because I went over the sergeant's head, he was not at all happy about me getting a second shot. He rode me even harder, but I was able to make it through this three week ordeal. Then it was

33

off to the academy in Tucson, AZ. The name of the academy is ALETA, which stands for Arizona Law Enforcement Training Academy. This is a live-in academy that is run like a military boot camp. When I arrived at the academy the drill sergeant was immediately on my case. I soon came to realize that he was yelling at me exclusively. Whenever we had to do more push-ups it was due to me failing. Everyone was also made to run to the water tower and back a lot. The other recruits were getting very ticked off over the extra work they had to put in on my behalf. To this day I can't say for sure that the sergeant in Mesa, AZ had anything to do with the extra dose of pressure I experienced, but I suspect he did. What I did next was the unthinkable! I resigned from the academy, and from Mesa Police Department. When I faced the sergeant, his statement was, "I knew you would never make it." He also told me, "As long as I'm in law enforcement, I will make sure that you never become a police officer." I was devastated and hurt! I would weep uncontrollably night after night. I was nearly inconsolable. What had I done? I couldn't take it back now. It's amazing what pressure and mind games will do to an individual. It can cause a person to throw away all their hopes and dreams in a heartbeat. Again I "Almost" had my dream job, but I let it slip through my hands. I would later ask myself what was learned from this time in my life. Even though the sergeant put every obstacle in my way,, I have only myself to blame for failing. At that time I was trying to do things by my own might, and thus I wasn't prepared to finish well. Psalm 29:11 says, "The Lord gives strength to his people; the Lord blesses his people with peace." Eventually, God gave me a peace about this situation. I have on many occasions prayed for this sergeant that God would touch his life. Peace is achieved when your disdain for someone is turned to love for someone who is lost. By no means can I honestly say I haven't asked the questions, "What if I would have just stuck it out? What would my life be like today?" If you're like me you have asked God on several occasions, "what if". I wish I could say that because this door was slammed by God that I didn't continue to bang my head against a wall trying to go down my own path. Nope, I was convinced that if the Lord opened this door, He would open another one soon! So I kept chasing the wind to get my "Almost" dream job.

I figured that since I had just resigned from a police department that my chances of getting hired on somewhere else were slim to none. Then I found out that the San Diego Police Academy had a program where a person could enroll and pay their way through. I had this burning need to prove I was not a quitter and that I could finish an academy. After a small background check to make sure I wasn't a criminal, I was allowed to sign up for the academy as an open enrollee. Open enrollees are required to do everything that the other cadets must do. The curriculum was the same for everyone. However, most of the cadets in the academy were sponsored by an agency, and were thus drawing a paycheck. Open enrollee's were required to pay for everything themselves through the entire 7½ month process. At that time I was sure that if I were to complete the academy, that surely some agency would see the chance to save money and hire me over someone who wasn't already certified. One day during the academy I "Almost" became a porcupine! We were doing vehicle chase training and vehicle stops. Well, on one of my vehicle stops the instructor got out of the car and ran. I gave chase around a

35

fence and into an open field. As I was chasing the suspect/instructor I tripped over a rock and fell into a cactus. It hurt a lot! Well, I was excused for the rest of this day from attending the academy. I had to go to the emergency room where an intern had to pick all of the prickles out, one at a time. She was using a microscope so thick and powerful that had it been outside it would have disintegrated every ant in the vicinity. Take it from me, stay away from cacti! Well, I finally obtained all of the necessary knowledge and skills to be police officer in the state of California. On June 26, 1992 I graduated with a P.O.S.T. Certificate. P.O.S.T. stands for Peace Officer Standards & Training. My certificate was good for three years, so surely, I thought, some agency would pick me up now. After all, I had vindicated myself from my past mistakes in Mesa, AZ. I had proven I had what it took to be a law enforcement officer. Soon and very soon, there would be no more "Almost" to getting my dream job.

Now fresh out of the academy with a certification, I sought to apply for a job with the San Diego Police Department. Again, I had proven I was good enough to make it through their academy. They would save money by hiring me, so logically I concluded this to be a wise move. At that time the department was only hiring reserve officers. The difference between a regular police officer and a reserve officer, is that a reserve officer has police power only while on duty. Additionally, they are not paid positions, but are required to put in a certain amount of volunteer hours each month. The process to become a reserve took about three months. The day I got the job and was sworn into this position was another very high moment in my life. This was as close to "Almost" as I had ever gotten. With this position I was able to ride with another officer in the capacity as a police officer. I was doing everything like a regular officer, just not getting paid to do it. It didn't bother me all that much because I was willing to put in my time to get to the next step, convinced that once the department saw that I was able to efficiently do the job, I would be hired on to full-time status. One day, I was notified that the department was finally hiring full time officers. Very excited, I put in my application in. The process to be a full-time officer was the same as becoming a reserve officer. Since I had just gone through this process to become a reserve officer, I felt this was just a formality and was not very concerned. Then another dreadful day came along. The reserves sergeant called me at home and told me to bring all of my stuff to the station. When I got to the station I was told they had to let me go. When I questioned him as to why I was being let go, I was told was that it was because of the "Garcia Act." To this day I have never found an attorney that could find this "Act." Anyway, supposedly I didn't pass something in the process to becoming a full-time officer, which meant that they couldn't keep me on as a reserve any longer either. If I had known that applying to become a full-time officer was going to risk my reserve status, I surely wouldn't have done it. Days of sobbing, hurt and sorrow followed. I questioned myself constantly. What could I have done different to change this outcome? I didn't do anything wrong to deserve this fate. I again "Almost" got my dream job! What principles did I learn from this? The people that were hired were just as qualified as I was to be in that job. There didn't seem to be any rhyme or reason why I was excluded. Then I was hit between the eyes with the following verse in Ecclesiastes 9:11 where it says, "I have seen something else under the sun: The race is not to the swift or the battle to the strong, nor does food come to the wise or wealth to the brilliant or favor to the learned: but time and chance happen to them all." What a powerful verse! It was right there in front of me smacking me in the face. That explains it all. A person's ability to attain any goal is more attributed to chance than our own planning. So who is in control of the chance happenings? The pat answer is God, right? If there was no sin in this world then I don't believe so many things would be left up to chance. Life would be a lot more fair without sin. Since this world as we know it today will never attain perfection, we as Christians need to be content with "Almost." Again, I wish I could stop here and tell you that I didn't keep hitting my head against the same wall!

Needing a job while yet still searching for a law enforcement job, I went back into Security work. I was hired on as an Armed Security Officer with Fairbanks Ranch in Rancho Santa Fe, CA. This is a highly affluent gated community. The homes were gorgeous, and the minimum price for a home was around one million dollars. While there I was able to do some police-type activities in an attempt to keep me current. There were strict rules within the community for parking, speeding, and other homeowner association violations. I was a patrol officer within this gated community. It was my job to make sure the rules were followed, and to keep people safe. Our patrol vehicles were equipped with radar, and we made traffic stops to issue citations to the residents.. On several occasions, we worked with the sheriff's department on cases that were more severe. Consequently, I felt I was staying active in my pursuit of my "Almost" dream job.

During the three years at Fairbanks Ranch, I put in over four hundred applications to various law enforcement agencies. I went through many writing tests, physical agility tests, oral interviews, background checks, and enough psychological tests to sink a thousand ships. Every time that I would get to the background phase I would get my hopes up again, only to be crushed. The emotional roller coaster ride I was on was taking its toll on me. If anyone reading this has beaten their head against the wall to get into a career as much as I have, then first I want to say that I'm sorry. Second, please reach out to me - I would love to speak with you. Remember that I'm a "type A" personality? God created me to be more stubborn than wise. I have actually prayed that God would remove this hunger inside me to do law enforcement. I would say, "God, if it's your will for me to be in law enforcement, then show me the right door to walk through," or, "Lord, if it's not your will, shove me with great force to the path I need to be on." Notice I used the word "shove," because that's what it was going to take. Three years finally rushed by with me simply "Almost" getting my dream job, which meant that my P.O.S.T certificate was no longer valid! All the time and money I spent going through the academy was now a waste. Did God really think it was a waste of time though? Let me give you a story about trees. If trees are faced with a heavy wind within the first year of being planted, they can easily blow down. However, if trees experience no wind at all during their first year of growth, as soon as a heavy wind comes along, they could also blow down. You see, light breezes against the trees cause them to grow their roots deeper into the soil. Later, when the big storm of life comes along, they are prepared to handle it.

You will see later in this book that some of the storms that came early in my life turned out only to be breezes, which were meant to get me deeply rooted for the real storms to come! Every "Almost" in life is God telling you to stay prepared for something big!

By the time I turned 25 years old I was exhausted from chasing my "Almost" dream job. Now I was married as well, and needed to settle down. The need for me to be practical about my career choice hit me square between the eyes. Don't get me wrong, I was a kicking and a screaming the whole time. It was a rough time in my life. How do I reconcile this burning desire to be in law enforcement, and yet move on with my life to take care of my wife? If you were to see my complete resume of the 26 jobs I have had, you would understand what chasing the wind is about. As a matter of fact, whenever I want to apply for a job, I put all of the paperwork for my previous jobs in a wheel barrel and take it with me. If an employer wants more than five years of employment history I ask, "How late are you willing stay?" I feel badly about all the trees that I have wasted in writing my jobs down. Wherever I worked I always gave a hundred percent, as if I was working for the Lord. Even so, my heart just wouldn't let go of its dream. I honestly believe that many people are also waiting to "Almost" get their dream job. Are you one of them?

So for the past 15 years I have been relegated to a jack of all trades, but a master of none. For a while I worked in Tijuana, Mexico as a buyer for a company with a funny name. Their name was "Hooker Headers." If you're into car racing, you will know that they made exhaust headers. This job was short lived, because Holley Industries bought them out. I owned my own car detailing company as well. With a 65 gallon water tank in the back of a Mitsubishi Mighty Max and a bunch of chemicals, I was set. Most of the vehicles were high end in nature. My wife helped with this venture. She would take care of the interior while I was taking care of the exterior. One of my fondest memories was detailing a 1947 original Woody on several occasions. It was hard to count on steady income from this business though. If it rained I couldn't work. Also, having your vehicle detailed is not the highest priority for most people. The cancellation rate is high in this business.

A good friend of mine was looking to build a huge gas station, hand car wash and convenience store. He took me under his wing and showed me the process from start to finish. We drove around looking for a good location. The land was eventually purchased, and an architect was then needed to draw up blue prints. Once the blue prints were completed, they had to be approved by the city, which, by the way, is a painful process! After that, contractors had to be interviewed for the construction job. Once it was built, vendors had to be interviewed, to determine whose items would be sold in the store. If you know anything about the beverage business, they will fight to the death to make sure they have the most space or the best door location in a store. To me it was pretty comical to see people fighting over such a petty thing. Once the store was stocked, we had to hire and train employees to work it. I believe I gained more experience working this job than any other job I've ever had. Unfortunately, I was working 60 to 70 hours per week, and that's not conducive to a good marital relationship. I needed to work to live, not live to work. This is the one job I could have seen as taking over and replacing my "Almost" dream job in life. Today I'm still convinced that if I ever had the funds to build my own station that I have acquired enough knowledge to make it happen. Even though this job didn't work out, I have remained good friends with the owner. Thank you for everything you imparted to me, Lawrence!

Most of my experience now lies in the insurance field. My first experience in this business was with AAA Insurance. I spent a little over three years with this company before moving to Arizona. One of the fun things about the insurance industry is how people get into accidents, and the ways they damage their property. The incidents and stories are always different. Due to so many different types of losses, the job was always interesting. One such story is just plain hilarious, so I must share it. A lady was making a claim for damages to her boat trailer. Obviously, we needed to know how it was damaged. She had recently bought this boat and when it was delivered to her it was on the trailer she purchased as well. Someone should have taken time to explain a few things about how the process worked. She took her boat out to Mission Bay to go boating for the first time. She kept giving the boat power, but it felt very sluggish. The boat didn't want to move very fast no matter how much power she gave it. At this time she was very frustrated, and seeing something was wrong, the harbor patrol came over to assist. Upon inspection from the harbor patrol, he turned to her and said, "Are these straps?" Without missing a beat she said, "Those are holding the trailer to the boat." The guy with the harbor patrol replied, "What?! You seriously have the trailer still hooked to the boat?" He couldn't compose himself and he started laughing out loud. He told her, "You have to remove the boat from the trailer first!" So the damages to the trailer were from dragging it on the bottom while attached to the boat. Now that's funny! Except for the past couple of years, I have worked in the management side of auto insurance. I even tried my hand at selling insurance for a year and a half. Then, as a result of the recent economic downturn, I was unemployed for 10 months. Later in the book I will explain what I have done to keep myself busy. Obviously, one of those things is writing this book.

After "Almost" one year of unemployment, God has answered my prayers (and the prayers of many others) When I was hired on with another insurance company. One of the wonderful benefits of this job, is that I am being given a company vehicle to drive. I had been worried that when I did get a job, my wife would not be able to get to her doctor appointments, since we had only one vehicle. Well, God took care of this need by supplying a job that comes with a car. I told the branch manager that hired me that my priorities in life are God, family, and then my job. He stated that he felt the same way. I hope this means he loves the Lord as well. This job came right as I finished writing this book. I came back to add this into the book because I felt it was important for others to see that God is still answering prayers today. He knew just how much time that I would need to be off of work to complete this book. I now pray that this door was opened up for me to be able to reach my new co-workers for Christ!

God created all of us to be creative beings. This means that work is a gift from God, not a curse. If we are more concerned with "Almost" getting our dream job than

getting the job God has for us then we're missing out! You
see, if the Lord wouldn't have moved me about to so many
different jobs, how would I have been able to meet the
people God placed in my life? If we are mindful to "work
to live", as opposed to "live to work", then we can become
as moldable putty in God's hands, as He will be able to
move us from this place to that place more freely. If God
would have given me my dream job instead of "Almost"
giving it to me, then my roots would have been entrenched
way too deeply to uproot. If we're all about ourselves and
what we want to do, then it's harder for God to get our
attention. God would still get our attention in the end, but
He would have to use more drastic measures to do so. Isn't
it easier to release it all to God in the first place? In Jonah
chapter 1: 1-3(a), "The word of the Lord came to Jonah son
of Amittai. 2 Go to the great city of Ninevah and preach
against it, because it's wickedness has come up before me.
3 But Jonah ran away from the Lord and headed for
Tarshish. He went down to Joppa, where he found a ship
bound for that port." Later, in verse 15, the crew throws
Jonah overboard due to the raging sea. In verse 17, the
Lord provides a great fish to swallow Jonah, and Jonah
remains inside this fish for three days and three nights.
This is a pretty harsh way for the Lord to get someone's
attention. He may not be as drastic as this today, but I
guarantee you that he is pursuing you still. If you "Almost"
get your dream job it should make you think, "maybe this is
a belly of the whale moment in my life. Am I where I
should be?" Once you're back on the right path, the Lord
will have the whale spit you out so that you can pursue
whatever it is that He has for you.. What should our dream
job look like? Anything that aligns with this scripture,
Mark 16: 15: "He said to them, "Go into all the world and

preach the good news to all creation." At "Almost" every job I have had, the Lord has brought someone into my life. That person had questions about God, or simply needed encouragement to continue the journey with God. God was doing the moving and the shifting of jobs in my life. If one day God opens the door for another law enforcement position, I would probably do that as well. However, I must let God do all things through me in his time, instead of allowing myself to chase after the wind. If God uses me to reach the lost for him, then "Almost" getting my dream job is worth the price! After all, Jesus paid it all for me first!

Chapter 3 "Almost" Didn't Marry My Wife

Before I begin the next three chapters, I feel that I should
prepare you to read them. These sections will be very
difficult for me to write. My plan is to lay bare my soul
and become completely transparent with you. You may
find a few people, maybe even a pastor or two that is
willing to be as open as I'm going to be with you. Imagine
if your pastor was completely open about their thoughts
and deeds, would you be understanding toward them? Be
honest. I believe in most cases, Christians would devour
them and throw them out of the church. Instead, we need
to take heed to what Matthew 7:3 says: "Why do you look
at the speck of sawdust in your brother's eye and pay no
attention to the plank in your own eye?" All of us have
planks in our eyes, but we are unwilling to be open about
them for fear of what others will think of us. That is the
issue. It's tough for anyone to be bare. The word "bare" in
itself seems to suggest that were naked. Why do we clothe
ourselves in the first place? Adam and Eve weren't
worried about being bare in the Garden of Eden until sin
entered the picture. When clothes were no longer optional,
neither were masks! In order for me to be bare with you, I
must remove the masks that I wear. Have you ever truly
removed your mask for all to see the good as well as the
ugliness in your life? Well, if you're like most people you
have no problem with having people see the good stuff.
When it comes to the ugly things we tend to stuff them
deep down. We tell ourselves lies that we're the only one
that has the thoughts we have -"Boy, if others knew the sin
in my life they would be ashamed of me..". I must tell you
that the majority of people have had the same thoughts that

I have had.   Satan does a great job at whispering lies into your ear. He says, "Don't tell people what you're thinking. Don't let others know of the sin in your life." You see, if Satan feeds you this lie enough then you start to believe it. Then we all go about our lives spiritually dead inside. Churches today are full of Christians that are deathly afraid of divulging any of their sin. I believe great revival can happen today in our churches if we're able to lay bare our souls to each other. A church that can do this will be freed from Satan's lies. Will this process be pain free? Nope! It will hurt an awful lot at first. I tell my kids that anything in life that is worth something takes work to achieve it. If it were easy then Satan wouldn't have such a strangle hold on so many people!   After all, what is a church really? It's a hospital for sinners. In Matthew 9:12 Jesus says, "It is not the healthy who need a doctor, but the sick." Do you want an alive, on-fire-for-God church? Stop listening to the whispers of the devil. Start taking off your masks and walk free with God! So with that being said, I have chosen to live free and bare my soul to you. I don't in anyway condone my thoughts or my deeds! I'm a sinner and without Christ dying for me I would be lost. I must constantly go to God with everything in order to stay close to him. So Lord, please speak through me as I write these chapters. Please use my "Almosts" to give this reader healing. In your name I pray these things. Amen!

In September of 1989 I met my [now] wife, Laura Presley. Well how did this meeting come about in the first place? My best friend Dan Kendall's mother, Mary, happened to be in a class with Laura. Mary knew that I was studying Administration of Justice in college, and that I wanted to be in law enforcement. So when Laura told Mary that she was studying the same courses and had the same aspirations, Mary got excited. She told Laura all about me and said, "You just have to meet him." Thank God for match makers like Mary. If it hadn't been for her, I'm convinced I would still be a lonely, single man today! After all, I had not had much luck with the ladies. My self-esteem was not even a blip on the radar screen! So Mary told me all about Laura that same day after her class. My interest was extremely peaked at this point. Mary proceeded to get Laura's phone number and asked if it was alright for me to call her. Laura jokes today that this was her first of many mistakes! I called her from Mary's home, and we began a long conversation that went on for at least an hour. Over the phone her voice sounded beautiful and sexy! Now visions of sugar plums were dancing in my head. I am just kidding, of course. Since neither I, nor Laura had much dating experience, Mary took it upon herself to help out. Also, Laura was a very shy person. Mary had a great idea to get us together. She called Laura up and invited her over to her house for dinner. This was a blind date with a little more of a comfortable feel to it. Being with someone she knew and not starting out alone with me gave her confidence. The date was set for five days later on a Saturday night. With all of the excitement, I didn't really sleep well. I had so much anticipation running around in my heart and mind! But there was no backing out now, as this life changing moment was set in motion!

The day of the blind date finally arrived. My stomach was churning and my hands were shaking. It was hard to not be nervous. I so very much wanted to make a good first impression. The day before our date, I had hurt my wrist, so I was wearing a brace. I thought for sure that Laura would see the brace and say, "What a geek!" I found out much later that the brace made me look like a wounded puppy, and it actually helped me! So I guess a little pain at the right time is a good thing. When Laura walked through the door to meet me my breath was taken away! She was so stunning. She was wearing a brown blouse with lions on it. Her pants were also brown, matching her blouse, and her shoes were cute brown boots. Her hair was flowing like the wind was blowing through it and her make-up was done perfectly – not too much, and not too little but just right. Still in shock, I gave her a rose to make a good impression. In my mind I was saying, "This beautiful woman is way out of my league." There was no way she would consider dating a guy like me. Remember, my self-esteem was horrible at this time of my life. I was decked out in my white pants, and a nice green shirt. It's funny how a moment in time over 20 years ago can still be so vivid today. At this time I would like to encourage you to take a minute to picture your spouse, the love of your youth. Close your eyes and get a mental picture of what your special loved one looked like the first time you met them. Was your heart beating fast? Obviously you must have felt this person was good looking, or you wouldn't have married them. I believe to have a healthy, long lasting relationship it's so important to take yourself back in time and remember those early thoughts and feelings. Alright, back to seeing Laura for the first time. To this day I remember what she was wearing, but I can't remember much of what was said. We sat down in the dining room next to each other at the table. I'm not actually sure what I had to eat that night, but I remember it being a good dinner. I must have been in some sort of a trance. A beautiful woman was sitting next to me and actually talking to me!

After dinner it was suggested that we play a card game called "Hearts." Now I do remember playing cards pretty vividly. Laura was a very competitive game player. Her wit, charm and personality really came out while she was playing. Also, she had an urge to win no matter what it took. To this day I still believe she cheated to win that night. She was the score keeper and it didn't add up right. Do you think it's any different today? Let's just say if you happen to play her in any game, make sure you keep score!

After the card game, it had gotten late, and I asked Laura if she had to be home yet. She said she didn't, so I asked her if she would like to take a ride to La Jolla to walk by the beach and get to know each other better. To my amazement she said that she would love to. My car at that time was a white 1985 Ford Mustang. Now the driver's seat was in good shape, however, the passenger seat – well, that's a different story. So I went to the passenger side of my car to open the door for her. Then I apologized for the seat being broken. (The passenger seat leaned horribly to the right.) It was embarrassing that here I had a beautiful woman on a date, and the chariot she was riding in was anything but comfortable. It's just so humorous to think about all the little things I was worried about back then. Don't we strive so much to make sure all of the details are perfect, instead of just enjoying each other's company? So when we got to the beach in downtown La Jolla, California, I got out of the car and walked around to open the door for Laura. If you're ever near La Jolla, I recommend you stop for a visit. It's so romantic! There is a jetty with a walk way that goes part way out into the ocean. During the day time there are seals all over the place. When high tide comes in, the waves actually break over the concrete jetty, and can get you soaked. The night Laura and I visited couldn't have been more perfect. It was a full moon that night. It was like God had turned on his big hundred watt light bulb just for us. We walked out to the end of the jetty and commented on the moonlight and stars. It was so beautiful that night. God's creation is always beautiful, but being with a gorgeous woman just brought it even more to life. We got there about thirty minutes before high tide. As we were out talking with each other the waves started getting higher and higher. Then a really big wave came out of nowhere and got us wet. I like to think it was God's way of cooling down the hot date! We both enjoyed talking and getting to know more about each other. It was time to whisk my princess back to Mary's house to end the date. It was a day that I never wanted to end. It was such a refreshing feeling to be paid attention to. Back at Mary's house I asked Laura if she enjoyed the date. She stated she had a lovely time with me. My next question was even scarier for me to ask - "Would you like to go on another date with me?" To my surprise, she said she would like that very much. I watched as Laura got into her VW Bug and drove off. Do you think I got much sleep that night? My head was spinning. What a day I just had! I couldn't wait until our next date!

Well I don't think I made it a complete twenty-four hours before calling her up again. It was about eight o'clock the next evening, and I called to see if she would like to go to a movie with me. She said she would love to do that. I went to her house and picked her up around 9PM. I didn't know this until a much later time, but her grandfather told me that she was in her pajamas already when I called. She got off the phone and quickly got dressed. She hurried to put make-up on to look good for me. Her grandfather also said she was absolutely giddy with excitement after I called. I guess she probably had the same fears as I did. What if the first date was the only date? Well, I don't even remember what we watched that night. At that point I was just enjoying the time I got to spend with her. Just talking to her meant everything to me. After that night we talked all the time. I don't even think a day went by that we didn't make time to see each other. After about two weeks of dating, I decided that I wanted to do something romantic again. So before our next date, I bought two red roses and I took Laura to dinner at a steak house. This is when I found out for the first time that she loves prime rib. She not only likes prime rib but she loves it as raw as you can get it. Talk about opposites! If my meat is not dead as dead can be I won't eat it. Poor Laura! Whenever we go out to eat steak I will tell them they can butterfly mine so my wife won't have to wait forever for her food. Once dinner was over I drove her up to the top of Mount Soledad. This is a mountain overlooks both Pacific Beach, and La Jolla. It has such a great panoramic view of the city and the lights are so beautiful from up there. While sitting on the steps below the cross, I decided it was time to make a bold move. We had seen each other almost every day for the past two weeks with no physical contact whatsoever. To say I'm a slow mover is an understatement. As a side note, if you are looking for a long-lasting, quality relationship, I believe you will be more apt to find one in the slow mover rather than in the quick one. I was a very shy person, and I also wanted to show the utmost of respect to Laura as well. I turned to Laura and asked her if I could hold her hand. To my delight she didn't turn me down. As I held her hand I had never felt closer to another person in my life. In my mind a fireworks show was going off. What a flood of emotions you feel when you actually touch another for the first time! Since I was scoring a thousand at that point, I asked her if she would be my girlfriend. She said, "I would like that very much." This was another night that I didn't ever want to end. At the end of the date, as we sate in the driveway of Laura's house, I asked her if I could give her a hug. Again, she didn't deny me. It was one of those hugs that again you could have fit four other people between the two of us. This was all so new to me. I always wanted to make sure I was a gentleman around Laura. I never wanted to put her in a position where she would feel uncomfortable. Well do suppose that now that I had held her hand and given her an "Almost" genuine hug, that I got a lot of sleep that night? Come on! You know the answer to that question by now. If not, where have you been?

Once Laura and I started dating, my life was "smooth sailing" - until we hit the three week pot hole. I had seen Laura just about every day for those three weeks. I didn't realize that in my need to love and be loved that I was smothering her. Again, my "type A" personality didn't know any other way. On the way to take Laura home on our three week anniversary, she dropped a bombshell on me. She said, "I don't want to see you anymore." My heart missed a few beats at that moment. Then she told me that I was smothering her, and that this was all going too fast. This was the first instance where I "Almost" didn't marry my wife! My response will probably shock you, but I turned to Laura and said, "I won't allow you to break up with me. I will do what it takes to keep you in my life." My belief was that she didn't really want to break up, but that she was scared. My commitment to her was that I

53

would slow things down. We would take things at a slower pace. I vowed to not call or see her every day. This "slow it down thing" only lasted about two weeks, before Laura began initiating the calls. I guess she just wanted to feel as though she was in control of the pace of the relationship. If you ask Laura, she will tell you that I grew on her "like a fungus."

By the time our relationship hit the four month mark I just knew I wanted to spend the rest of my life with Laura. Now Laura wasn't a believer in Jesus at this time. I thought in my infinite wisdom that I could just change her myself. But it doesn't work that way with God. Thank the Lord Laura did give her life to Jesus, but that didn't happen until about four years down the road. Remember, I grew up in the church. I knew exactly what God says about dating an unbeliever. In 2 Corinthians 6:14 it says "Do not be yoked together with unbelievers. For what do righteousness and wickedness have in common? Or what fellowship can light have with darkness?" Love will sure blind you from the truth! Satan loves it when our desires start to take control instead of our trust in God's way of doing things. This wasn't Laura's fault by any means. Being a non-Christian meant that she was not held to the same standard as I was as a believer. Nothing that God tells us in the Scriptures is meant to kill our joy. It's meant to protect us from destroying ourselves from within. In my mind I always played down the fact that she wasn't saved. I rationalized that she was a good person, and thus, it was alright. Do you ever rationalize your sin with God? It's the start of a slippery slope when we let our mind ponder on our needs instead of what God desires for us. At the fifth month of our relationship I made the big purchase. I bought an engagement ring with what little money I had saved up. It wasn't a big ring, about a ¼ carat. I then started formulating a plan in my mind to choose the best time and place to propose marriage. Our six month anniversary was here and I decided this would be the big day! I took Laura out to the same steak house as we went to in the start of our relationship. How could Laura tell me "no" with a good rare prime rib steak in her belly? After dinner I took her back to downtown La Jolla to the jetty that goes out into the ocean. Funny enough, it was at about high tide again and the waves were crashing over the jetty already. This meant that I had to hurry! So we quickly went to the end of the Jetty. I turned and faced Laura, got down on one knee, and asked her if she would spend the rest of her life with me. Obviously, she said "yes" and I put the engagement ring on her finger. Of course, there was some lip locking going on, but I will leave some of that up to your imagination.

Now that I was engaged to be married to this wonderful woman, my mind was not focused on the ways of God. At that time, Laura's grandparents, who raised her since she was 12, had two homes in Mission Valley. The home right next door to them was where Laura's dad and mom used to live. When Laura was 12 years old, her dad split up from her mom. Shortly thereafter, her mom was diagnosed with terminal cancer. Approximately six months later, Laura's mother passed away. When Laura turned 18 years old, her Grandparents let her live in the home next door – the one that she had lived in with her parents. When I say next door, it was literally attached by a porch, so that you could take 5 steps from one house to the other. Because she lived on her own, it was easy to fall into sin. I was still doing a paper route at this time, and I would stay over at Laura's house until 2a.m. Then Laura would come with me to help me deliver the papers. Being 20 years old and unmarried, I plunged into a sinful life style. We each gave each other our treasure, which should have been saved for the marital bed! God only gives each person one treasure like this. Once it's gone we can never get it back! 1 Corinthians 6:18 says, "Flee from sexual immorality. All other sins a man commits are outside his body, but he who sins sexually sins against his own body." So what was going through my mind at that time? Why would I give my treasure away before marriage? At the time the devil was doing a lot of whispering in my ear. He would say things like, "You're already engaged to be married. After all, this is the women you're going to spend the rest of your life with. This person that will be your first will also be your last, so indulge yourself." Once you let yourself get into a compromising position, it's hard to turn from the sin at hand. Again, I grew up in church, so I knew what I was doing was wrong. Yet, I couldn't resist sin's temptation. Here is some advice for you, because I believe everyone's mind works similarly in this area. At the beginning of a relationship, you simply talk, and get to know each other. You're scared to make any physical contact with the other person. Then one day you hold that person's hand. It's a huge major step in the process of your relationship. You say to yourself, "That wasn't so bad. After all, holding her hand is not a sin." Then one day you kiss the other person. Again it's exhilarating, and almost taboo. The mind kicks in again with its rationalizing skills –"Hey, that's not too bad. It's not sin, and I can stop myself." Things continue until the next thing you know, you've given away the treasure that God gave you to hold onto until marriage. It all happens so fast. I believe that you can get to know someone well enough to make a marital decision without ever making physical contact in the first place. Although, since I didn't take this road, it may be easier said than done. I'm just saying that once you start walking down this path, the devil is getting happier the whole way!

By this time, for all practical purposes, we were living together. I think my Dad and Mom might have been in denial about it for awhile. However, once I got hired in Mesa, AZ and we moved out there together, it would have been be hard for anyone to deny the type of relationship we were in. We got a one bedroom one bath apartment together. The world was just perfect at that time, so I thought! We were in Arizona for about a year before we moved back to San Diego. Once back in San Diego we got an apartment together in Mira Mesa. We just kept living in sin with no consequences for our actions. However, when we returned to San Diego, we also started to attend my home church again. Living with someone you are not married to is hard to keep secret at church. I think it must have been flashing at the back of the church in neon lights. "Hello church, did you know that Dale and Laura, on the right side of the church in pew #9, are living in sin?!" One day, the pastor called and said he wanted to speak with me. Notice he wanted to speak with me, not the both of us. He was calling my Christian walk into account, but couldn't hold my fiancé to the same standard. So I went to church, and had a conversation with the pastor.

The talk with the pastor was very cordial. He had a tough job at hand. He loved me and my finance, but couldn't look upon our sin without confronting it. He pointed out the scriptures I listed above, and so many more. I knew all of this already. He wasn't telling me something that I wasn't already aware of. I remember actually giving the pastor the reasons why it was alright for us to live together. Looking back I'm surprised he didn't burst out laughing at my trying to rationalize to him that my sin was different than everyone else's sin. I was trying to assure the pastor that we would get married soon, so he wouldn't worry about us. Once married, all would be right in God's eyes. What the pastor did next made me very angry at that time. It was only later in life that I came to realize that this man was truly a man of God. He was willing to use tough love on me. He was willing to go where most people don't have the guts to go. He had scripture on his side, and wasn't afraid to use it. The pastor said, "I love you very much, but I can't allow you to continue in this sin." He said that we needed to live separately immediately, but that he would be willing to give us marital counseling. Once he was sure that our marriage was grounded on God's principles, he would marry us. However, he stated that if we chose not live separately from each other, that I was not welcome to attend church there until I dealt with my sin. You see, he never said anything that was not biblical. He loved the person, but hated the sin. If I was willing to walk away from my sin, he was their willing to walk hand in hand to restore me. Since I had been unwilling to turn, repent and change my ways, he had to take a stand. What a righteous, Godly man he is. To tell you the truth, I haven't seen a lot of this going on in our churches today. I could probably write a whole book on this subject alone. We as Christians need to do a better job at showing love, but at the same time holding the line on sin. We need to be willing to confront others' sins, instead of changing our own value systems to tolerate the sin around us. For you see if we don't confront the sin, then were actually condoning it! God can't look upon sin, and it should make us sick to our stomachs to see the sin in our own church. Love the person first. Confront the sin second. Part ways if they refuse to listen. Proverbs 27:17 says, "As iron sharpens iron, so one man sharpens another." Iron is a very tough metal. It takes two very tough metals to come together to make each of them sharp. Likewise, it takes very tough Christians to brush up against other Christians to keep the church healthy and sharp! Pastor, thank you for kicking us out of the church. No one has ever showed so much love and concern for my soul as you did in that moment.

Dear reader, I feel it's important to take a quick side step in this chapter. Writing this book the past two days has been extremely difficult. Two nights ago, my mind was racing with wild thoughts. I don't think I got more than five hours of sleep. Then last night it was even worse! I was laying in bed feeling spiritually attacked. The best way I know how to describe it, is that it was like having God sitting on one shoulder, and Satan on the other. My mind was filling up with thoughts like, "You can't write this book. You're no good! You ought to be ashamed of yourself for digging up all of the past sins, and putting them down on paper. No one wants to read what you're writing." A feeling of worthlessness came over me. It was as if Satan was saying, "Look at all of the sins in your life. People are going to mock you for writing this stuff down." I fell asleep at around midnight, but I was very restless. I awoke again at 2:20 a.m., feeling under attack again. I forced myself back to sleep around 3:30a.m., only to be awakened again around 4:40 a.m. with more spiritual attacks. Finally, I

couldn't take anymore of the thoughts swirling around in my mind. Right then I prayed. "Lord, I'm so troubled by the thoughts racing in my mind. In your name, Jesus, I pray that Satan would leave my thoughts immediately." Once I was done praying this prayer I felt a peace come over me and the negative thoughts were gone. Then a verse popped in my head like it was being spoken directly to me. It was Psalm 103:12. The way I heard, though, was slightly different than it appears in the scriptures - it was more personal in nature. Here is this verse the way the bible reads: "As far as the east is from the west, so far has He removed our transgressions from us." Now this is how I heard this verse in my head: "As far as the east is from the west, so far have I removed your transgressions from you." The word "your" and the ending of "you" was so personal. This was a moment when I "Almost" gave up writing this book. Satan doesn't want this book to be written, because he knows that it might result in its readers having a closer relationship with the living God. Well, thank you for letting me take this side track. I just felt it was important to give you a peek into my mind as I struggle to get what God wants done down on paper. I pray that if you come under attack spiritually while reading this, you ask Satan to leave you alone in Jesus name. Don't let Satan win, and cause you to
only "Almost" read the rest of this book.

Now I would like to pick back up with the theme of this chapter. When I first met Laura she was the most beautiful women on the face of the planet. However, soon after getting engaged to be married, she began to have a big weight problem. Her actually weight was not the issue, so much as the thoughts that it caused me to have. It was very tough to wrap my head around the weight gain. At first I took it very personally. Here I was, trying to stay in good shape for her, yet she was letting herself go. Didn't she realize that men are stimulated more visually than women? Since I'm a visual creature, I needed her to be in better shape. I am in no way condoning my thoughts, I am just sharing them, in case others have found themselves in a similar situation. Growing up, I always had a picture of what my ideal wife would look like. Laura was nowhere close to that image any longer. I wasn't looking for Ms. America, or even a model type. I did, however, want a woman that kept herself in good shape. Even worse, when guys my age saw us together, they said hurtful things like, "Surely that's not your girlfriend", or, "Come on, Dale, you can do better than that!", or "You don't have to settle, you're still young." It never amazes me how Satan sees an opportunity to get a foothold in my life, and employs others to come alongside to help fester it along. Another issue that arose, was that the more weight that Laura put on, the less I wanted to be intimate with her. My attraction to Laura was based on outer beauty, not the beauty God sees. To this day, Laura has the kindest most beautiful heart of anyone I have ever met. But when you're 20 going on 21, and already living in sin, the beauty of someone's heart is not always what you are looking at.

So why did I stay with Laura if I wasn't happy? After all, we weren't married yet, so I could have broken it off, right? Well, when you accept Christ into your life, it's not as easy to call it quits on a non-believer. Satan on one shoulder gave me all the reasons why I was justified in leaving Laura. I considered doing just that on many occasions, due to her weight. This is the second example of how I

"Almost" didn't marry my wife. I knew that before making a decision to leave Laura, that I should seek Godly counsel. And I knew that if I did, they would ask if I'd been intimate with Laura outside of marriage. Of course the answer was "Yes, I have sinned against God, and continue to do so." The Godly counsel would then say that because of this we must get married. Envisioning this scenario, I felt that the only way to make this sinful situation right in the eyes of God was to marry Laura. In addition to that, I felt like I had God on my other shoulder saying, "Dale you're living in sin, and I the Lord your God am not pleased." So even though I wasn't on the correct path as a believer at that time, God's scripture was still ever present in my life. In my life I have always been true to my word to a fault. I'm the one that asked Laura for her hand in marriage. I'm the one at fault for taking her virginity away. All around me are people that throw away women like pieces of trash when they aren't happy with them any longer. The internal fight that raged in my soul was awful. There just aren't enough words or ways to explain the hurt I felt at that time. Why am I telling you this? Because if you're not married yet, then this pain can be avoided in your life by simply living by God's principles! God said don't commit fornication. That means don't have sexual intimacy with another outside of marriage. The intimacy outside of marriage might feel as good as the intimacy within marriage. However, when you jump the gun and do it contrary to God's ways, I guarantee that you will be in for a long hurtful road. I'm not saying that God can't restore everything in a couple's life, the way he has for Laura and I. However, if you can take God's road and avoid the pain that follows disobedience, I pray you do it!

Another reason I was staying with Laura is that I had all of the benefits of being married, and none of the responsibility. Because Laura's mother passed away when she was young, I knew that she was due an inheritance when she turned 21 years of age. That amount she received was $150,000. This wasn't a small amount of money. I have spent many nights weeping over how stupid we were with what God entrusted to us. Growing up, I had all of my needs provided for, but we didn't have a lot of money. Being 22 and 21 years old, we had no clue what to do with this money. Nothing in all my schooling prepared me to handle money. At the time we thought it was such a gift to have this money bestowed on Laura. But in reality, it was the worst thing that could have possibly happened. I hear stories all the time about how lottery winners wish they would have never won. Eventually they become broke and worse off than they ever were before. In my world this kind of money was going to last forever. If I would have put it in the bank back then, I would "Almost" have a million today!

In the end, this amount of money did more to tear Laura and I apart than it did to unite us. In Matthew 6:24 it says, "No one can serve two masters. Either he will hate the one and love the other, or he will be devoted to the one and despise the other." You cannot serve both God and money. It can't get much clearer than that verse. Today I hear people tell me that it's possible for someone to be rich, and be close to God. My response is it's surely possible, but not all that likely. Matthew 19:24 states, "Again I tell you, it is easier for a camel to go through the eye of a needle than for a rich man to enter the kingdom of God." Some people think the eye of a needle referred to in this verse is like a sewing needle. The entrance into a dwelling in biblical times was referred to as the needle. In other words, the verse is saying that it is easier for a camel to walk into your house, than for a rich man to enter the kingdom of God." I was serving the wrong master. I was seeing dollar signs instead of the signs of God in my life. It's sad to think how quick we were to give up the eternal riches and treasures that Christ had in store for us, in order to have a temporary good time then.. Has money ever been a stumbling block in your life? Even though I knew the verses above, I was still ensnared by Satan's lure. Money became a huge stumbling block in my life.

Almost immediately after getting the money, we were off to Las Vegas. We signed up for the Mirage Club. The perks were nice - spend enough money, and get free dinners. The whole glitter and lights were enough to put anyone in a trance. Blackjack was my game, and Laura enjoyed the $1 dollar slot machines. Some days we were up as much as five thousand dollars, and others we were down even more. The way the casinos lock a person into that lifestyle is by allowing you to win sometimes. In the end, the losing always outweighs the winning, but your brain only sees the possibilities of winning. Laura and I returned at least once a month to Las Vegas. I was there so much, I could have gotten a job as a tour guide. Taxi drivers and casino staff knew me by name. That's never a good thing! Soon I started to read every blackjack book and gambling book I could get my hands on. My life became about how I could win in Las Vegas. What a sad existence, using the talents God gave me for my own selfish way! They don't call it Sin City for nothing. It's sad that despite having a title like that, people will still flock there by the hoards!

Along with the gambling, we decided that we had to have a
new vehicle. We found a brand new 1992 Ford Ranger
XLT that had all the bells and whistles. We just had to
have it, so we paid cash on the spot for this vehicle. About
six months later, with only a little over 10,000 miles on the
car, something associated with the shifting broke. The part
wasn't covered, because it broke all the time on other
vehicles. So being very perturbed, we decided to trade it
in, rather than pay the $1,000 to have it repaired. In just six
months, we lost half the value of the car. We then went
and bought an Infiniti G20, paying for it outright as well.
The more I bought, the greedier I became, and the more I
felt entitled to purchase nice things. My life was spiraling
out of control. It took about a year and a half to burn
completely through Laura's inheritance. We just couldn't
stop our gambling ways. We were both addicted at this
point. Another horrible thing in this world is the credit
card. When you have money, lenders are so willing to
extend you whatever credit you want. It's just too easy to
get credit these days. Credit is never the way to go, unless
you are using it to make a house payment. If you can't
afford to buy something with cash, you simply shouldn't
buy it.

By the time Laura and I had been together for four years,
we were in debt over $80,000 dollars! If you don't think
this put an even bigger strain on our relationship, you're
wrong. With this insurmountable debt and no relief in
sight, I wanted to call the relationship off again. This is the
3rd instance of "Almost" not marrying my wife. What kept
me from breaking up this time? All of the same reasons as

before, plus the guilt about this new sin that I chose to be involved in. I felt very responsible for blowing Laura's inheritance! How would I ever make it up to her? If I left her, how was she going to take care of all of the debt that we racked up together? I just couldn't bring myself to leave her in the position that I helped her get into. The longer you live with someone outside of marriage, the harder it is to break it off, even if you want too. All of this was because of the sin in my life. I had let myself go so far off the path which Christ wanted for me. I was not going to church, or reading the word, or even praying to God. Yet God never left me. He was always there in the same spot – it was I who had turned my face away from Him, because I thought I could do it better on my own. I'm here to tell you that no one can do it by themselves. If God is not filling you up, then something else is. Revelation 3:15-16 says, "I know your deeds, that you are neither cold nor hot. I wish you were either one or the other! So, because you are lukewarm neither hot nor cold I am about to spit you out of my mouth." I was desperately trying to live my life on the fence. I was that lukewarm Christian. God says at the end of the verse, "I'm about to spit you out of my mouth." Thank you, Lord that even though I know you were about to spit me out, you never did. Thank you for your forgiveness!

My relationship with Laura hit a major hurdle at about the four year mark. People would always ask me when we were going to get married. "You've been together for four years - don't you think it's time?" Some of my responses to these questions were hurtful and ignorant. I would say things like, "Why buy the cow when I get the milk for free?" When you live with someone without being married, the urgency to get married just isn't there. Why should it be, when I have all of the benefits of being married already? In my mind, not being married gave me an easy bailout, out if needed. Even so, the thoughts that circled through my head were vicious. Since my self esteem was always low, I wondered if I just settled on the first woman that said "I love you." I also wondered if I could attract another woman. My brain even let me think that maybe this wasn't the woman that God wanted me to marry.

I had a female friend (we'll call her Sarah) that I had known since high school. One night while Laura was at work, Sarah came over to my apartment. Sarah wasn't sure if she should marry the man she was engaged to.. She told me she had the same questions in her mind as I did about marrying her fiancé. Having two people together alone questioning the same thing spelled disaster!! It started with just a kiss. I could feel both our hearts racing. The whole time my mind was saying, "This is wrong, turn back now!" However my body was saying that it felt so good to be held and caressed by another woman. My mind and body were constantly in conflict with each other that night. The next thing I knew, I was in my bed being intimate with another woman. This was and still is today the only other women I shared my treasure with. Oh how I wish I could take back that night, and say that my now wife was the only one. This night caused the biggest instance of "Almost" not marrying my wife.

Life as I knew it would forever be altered due to that moment in time. I had never felt more ashamed or guilty in my entire life. How could I betray Laura like that? My sin lifestyle was out of control. Immediately after this sin took place, we both felt an immense amount of guilt and remorse for what we had just done. Sarah took a very long shower. Not sure why it was so long - I never asked. I can guess it's because she felt ashamed as well, and was somehow trying to cleanse herself of this guilt. After her shower, she got dressed and we didn't say much to each other. This night altered the deep respect and friendship we previously enjoyed together. This one night was not worth losing a friendship over. Let me repeat this: ONE NIGHT OF PLEASURE IS NOT WORTH IT!!

Later that night when Laura got home from work, I told her that we needed to sit down and talk. She knew something was wrong. Maybe she was thinking that I was going to break up with her. Whatever she was thinking, I'm pretty sure she never thought I would betray her trust like I had.. As I was in the middle of the sin, I thought that I really didn't need to tell Laura. What she didn't know wouldn't hurt her. But the hurt that filled the deepest part of my soul was too much to bear. Because I respected, loved Laura deep down, I couldn't withhold this betrayal. I poured my heart out to Laura. I said, "I'm deeply sorry for hurting you. This feeling I have is awful I wish I could take it back." We both wept a lot that night. Laura had every right to end the relationship with me at that moment. This told me a lot of the deep love that Laura had for me. We slept in separate rooms for at least two weeks. When I did get back into the same bed with Laura, we didn't talk, and we were turned facing opposite directions. The initial process of healing probably took about three months, but the overall hurt will last for a lifetime. Just to bring up the name of "Sarah" in this book is going to dredge up memories that we both wanted to keep in the past. What a wonderful, strong, forgiving woman Laura is. To this day, she is still so quick to forgive me when I have wronged her. Even though she wasn't a believer in Christ at that time, I saw in her a lot of qualities of what a Christian should be. As a matter of fact, I was seeing more Christ-likeness in Laura than in my own self. This made me all the more miserable that I betrayed her. I should have known better. This should never have even come close to "Almost" happening! Since I wasn't walking very close to God at this time in my life, it was very easy for Satan to drag me down. Laura, thank you for your forgiveness! Thank you Jesus for your forgiveness, and for letting me know that I was someone that still had value, even despite my sinful choices.

After being together for nearly five years, Laura started to push me more heavily into getting married. She gave me an ultimatum that if I didn't marry her, she would leave me. She was never this forceful before. However, she was totally in the right for being pushy. I had dragged my feet for nearly five years. She had every right to say, "Hey Dale, if you're going to marry me then do it. At least I will know where I stand." This was a side of Laura I had never seen before. Somewhere deep inside she must have been tired of the sin and the hurt that was being caused by not being married. When she found out that my best friend Dan Kendall was going to be in town at the end of December, she said that it would be a perfect time to get married. Laura knew that when I got married, I wanted Dan to be my best man. So I called Dan, and he said he would be delighted to be my best man.

Off to the pastor of my church to make plans on getting married. The pastor said that we would have to go through Christian marital counseling with him first. Laura wouldn't agree to this stipulation, because she was still not a Christian herself. What happened next caused me to be angry with the church. The pastor refused to marry us for the following reasons: Neither of us wished to have Christian counseling,. we lived together before marriage, Laura was still not a believer, so we would have been unequally yoked, and the final reason, which makes me chuckle today, is that he stated that he refused to marry a couple that would not stay married forever. Looking back at what the pastor said and did that day, I would have to say that he is a strong, Godly man. Most pastors don't have this kind of conviction. If they are getting paid to marry someone, they will do it. Just think about it. My family had been going to this church for "Almost" thirty years up to this point. The pastor was sure risking a lot by saying he would not marry us. I actually wish more pastors would have this much love and conviction about marriage. This pastor took marriage so seriously, that he staked his reputation on not performing it on our behalf. At the time I will honestly say, I had much distaste for this pastor. But like anything in life, when you have time to reflect and see their decision through God's eyes, you come to realize he was right. But every year that goes by, I point out to him that we're still married. Just a little jab, but I'm sure he is delighted he was wrong in this instance.

With no pastor to marry us, and my friend only in town for a short time, it was looking like I would "Almost" not marry my wife again. As time was running out I came into contact with a friend that was a San Diego Police Officer.

He said that a reserve officer that he knew was also a pastor of a Lutheran church in Lemon Grove, CA. He called this pastor for me. The pastor said the date we wanted was open, and he just wanted to meet with us one time. So Laura and I met with this pastor. He did not have the same requirements as my home church pastor did, in order to marry us. To be honest, though, I wish he would have. In fact we only had to pay $150.00 for his services, the church and the reception hall. Laura also wanted to have champagne, and to do a money dance. Both of these were approved as well. So the rush was on. Laura got a beautiful wedding dress. I just wore a nice suit that I had. We put the whole thing together on a shoe string budget, because we were still in major debt at that time. Invitations went out to about two hundred people. I remember most of the people that attended our wedding. The guest that stands out in my mind the most though, was the pastor that refused to marry us.. It felt like he was still cheering us on, even though he felt it would have been wrong for him to marry us. On December 31st, 1994, there now was no more "Almost" about it - we were pronounced man and wife.

You're probably wondering whether Laura knows that I'm writing this all down. I assure you that I read all of this to her as I go along. Does it produce pain, dredging this stuff up? You bet it does. Laura's and my hope is that through our pain, you will either avoid making our mistakes, or you will find healing, if it's too late to avoid. Laura had many struggles that "Almost" caused us not to marry. You see the hurt and the sin in both of our lives. I hope you're able to see the pain that is caused when you fall off the path God wants for your life. If you are married, or are thinking about getting married, I would like to give a plug for a book that could tremendously help you.. I came across this book after being married for 10 years, and I wished I would have read it much sooner. The title of the book is "His Needs Her Needs: Building An Affair-proof Marriage" by Willard f. Harley Jr. This book offers a Godly perspective on the five major needs of men versus women. It shows that if you concentrate on meeting your mate's needs, and never worry about your own needs, your marriage will be affair-proof. I hope you see from reading this chapter that just because you may really blow it badly, and you're up to your eye balls in sin, that God still loves you! The Lord still uses the moments that we're not even "Almost" doing his will to bring us back into a right relationship with Him. Reader, do you ever think that you have done so much wrong that God doesn't love you? Do you ever think that God is done using you? If you're not on the path right now following God, he is out stretching his hand for you to come back. All you have to do is repent of your ways, and turn your face towards Him again. I will leave you with this scripture that demonstrates that God is not done with you yet. Psalm 139:13-16 says, "For you created my inmost being; you knit me together in my mother's womb. 14 I praise you because I am fearfully and wonderfully made; your works are wonderful, I know that full well. 15 My frame was not hidden from you when I was made in the secret place. When I was woven together in the depths of the earth, 16 your eyes saw my unformed body. All the days ordained for me were written in your book before one of them came to be." God wonderfully made you and me. He saw you and me while we were yet being formed. And all of my days were ordained for me before one of them came to be. God doesn't create junk. If God created you he has big audacious pre-ordained plans for your life. God is waiting to put you back into the game again. Don't sit on the sidelines any longer!

Chapter 4 "Almost" lost my wife to Cancer.

Dear reader, if you're about to tackle this chapter all at one time you may want to get yourself in a comfortable position. This has been one of the largest chapters in my own life, so putting it down on paper won't be any different. This journey has taken me and Laura through a great testing period for "Almost" ten years. A verse that comes to mind when I think about all of the testing that we have both have gone through is 2 Corinthians 4:7-10. It says, "But we have this treasure in jars of clay (some translations use earthen vessels) to show that this all surpassing power is from God and not from us. 8 We are hard pressed on every side, but not crushed; perplexed, but not in despair, 9 persecuted, but not abandoned; struck down, but not destroyed." Why does this verse mean so much to us? Well first we are all just jars of clay. Even though we are wonderfully made by God, this body we have is so fragile. If you drop a jar of clay it would most likely break. Our bodies on earth are decaying from the moment are born. Our bodies were made fragile so that we would be dependent on God's all surpassing power not on our own might. We really need to be praying to God everyday for the healthy times, and the unhealthy times. Our health is totally dependent on God. In verse 8 it states that we're hard pressed on every side. Talk about the feeling of pressure…having a loved one with cancer feels like the world is caving in around you. When bad news is delivered we feel like we're being persecuted and struck down. Even though we are struck down, we can't let it keep us down. We seek strength from God, and others to keep up the fight. The final part of that verse says, "but were not destroyed." If when we pass away in this earthly body, we know Christ as our personal savior, we can never be destroyed! My wife and I have been traveling on a very tough road for many years now. .So let me take you back in time, so that we can experience this long journey together.

In October of 2000, my wife took a nasty fall down a flight of stairs. At the bottom of those stairs she took a blow to her head. Laura said that right before the fall she was light headed and dizzy. I immediately drove her to the emergency room to be checked out. The doctors did a routine exam, drawing blood, and taking a CAT scan of her head. The doctor stated that all of the tests came back normal. Were still not sure today if the fall was caused by something the physician missed, or if the fall set into motion what would soon happen in her head. However, when we later tried to get a copy of the CAT scan from that first day, it had mysteriously vanished from the records department.

About a month later, Laura started to complain of very sharp headaches. The headaches were so painful; she had to lie down in a dark room and pain medication barely took the edge off. At first the headaches only came every couple of days, and lasted for about one hour During this time, Laura was also about 3 months pregnant. One day, her condition almost caused her to fall down another set of stairs, but I was there to catch her. We both agreed something was not right and we returned to the emergency room. After waiting an aggravating 6 hours to be seen the physician, he diagnosed Laura as having a terrible head cold and sent us away with a prescription for cold medicine. It must have been a horrible cold, because it just wouldn't go away. It felt as if the only "cold" we got was the cold shoulder from the doctors, just trying to give us a quick answer, and move us along.

At this time, both I and Laura worked at the same company. One day in the early part of January (about three months after the onset of the headaches) an employee came running over to my desk. I could see the terrified look on her face. She told me to come quickly because something was very wrong with Laura. When I got to Laura's desk, I noticed that she was staring straight ahead. She was trembling, and couldn't talk. All of her motor skills were completely shut down. I kept saying, "Laura! Laura! Can you hear me? What is happening?" I was very scared, because she wouldn't respond. Finally, about 15 minutes later, she came out of the seizure and started talking again. I was permitted to leave work to take Laura back to the emergency room. I should have learned my lesson by now, but what other alternative did I have at that moment?? The emergency room doctor said that this is something that can occur when a woman is pregnant and that it was really nothing to worry about. We left again, this time racking up another 8 hours in the ER. I was there so. often, I should have had a name badge and time card.

Laura was still having horrible, debilitating headaches. I told her she should make an appointment with her normal doctor to see if the ER doctor had missed anything. A few days later, she went to see her primary care physician. This person deserves a lot of credit, because she saw something that no one else did.. She used a small pen light to look into

Laura's eyes while the light in the room was off. There is a saying that the eyes are the window to the soul. This Dr. could see Laura's soul. She also noticed pressure behind Laura's eyes. This is usually the result of something in the brain causing swelling, and pressure. She referred us immediately to a neurological specialist, to get an MRI (Magnetic Resonance Imaging) . This was a more precise way of scanning the brain. So two days later we had an appointment to get this scan done for Laura.

When Laura arrived for her MRI, they instructed her to put on a gown and lie down on a special all-metal bed. As she lay down on this metal bed she said, "Wow this thing is freezing cold!" A registered nurse came in to explain what was about to happen. He said he had to start an IV so that a special dye could be inserted into her vein. This special dye is meant to go through her brain, so the MRI equipment can pick up different contrasts in her brain. The best way to explain contrasts is that cancer, or lesions, will show up as lighter colors than the rest of the brain tissue. Once the dye was injected into Laura's vein, they hit a button that slowly sent the metal table into a big white tube. Then a technician came into another room to start the MRI machine. This is not a quiet machine. It makes a "vroom" sound over and over again, as something inside the machine goes around and around taking pictures. The pictures taken by an MRI are like many thinly cut pieces of paper. Each picture shows a slightly different slice of the brain. . The technician asked Laura to remain very still during the test, which lasted for about an hour. It made her feel claustrophobic laying inside the tube for so long. Once the test was over, the technician said the scans would be turned over to the neurologist for review. They would call us if they saw anything worrisome, but otherwise, no news was good news.

On January 14th, I received a call at work from the neurologist, telling me that I needed to bring Laura in to see him the next day. I thought it was odd that he called me, and requested that I be there at the appointment with her. He also said that per his request, she shouldn't drive. I went to my supervisor, and he agreed that it was weird that they requested that I go with her. He also granted me the time off to take care of Laura. I immediately told Laura that the neurologist had called, and told her what he said. We both agreed that it didn't sound good. We couldn't concentrate on anything at work the rest of that day, and neither of us got any sleep that night.

January 15th, 2001 is a date that is very engrained in my brain, and forever etched into every fiber of my being. When Laura and I entered the neurologist's office that day, we were immediately introduced to a woman named Karen from hospice. We hadn't even looked at the scan, or gotten diagnosis yet, and this doctor was introducing us to hospice. Hearing the word "hospice" made both of us frightened. Anyone who has ever known someone with cancer knows that they only gets involved in the process when time is drawing to a close. Still in shock, we were taken to a room that was set up with large white boxes on the wall. These boxes have a back light to them, allowing you to view the scan. The Neurologist clipped the scans to the boxes. We had to view a lot of different MRI scans. It would have been neat if we had these boxes to see family photos - having to view pictures of my wife's brain is not nearly as fun!

The diagnosis from the neurologist was a mouthful for him to say. It took me even longer to do all of the research on what it was. Here is the long, scary name of what my wife is dealing with. It's called an Oligodendroma Astrocytoma Blastoma Grade III (although we didn't actually know the grade of the tumor at that point). The Dr. took his pen out, and started to point to the tumor with the big ugly name. He showed us a highlighted area about 5 centimeters in diameter. We timidly asked what we were looking at. He said that it was a large mass growing inside Laura's brain. We asked where in the brain this tumor was located. He told us that it was attached to the speech, and logic part of the brain. The seizures Laura was having was due to the pressure on the speech portion. The news that day was getting worse and worse. You might ask how it's possible to deal with such tragic news. All I can say is that God will never give you more than you can handle. At times it felt like we were both hanging off a cliff! However we weren't falling, because God had us by the back of the neck, holding us up through this very trying time. In your most desperate moments, fix your eyes upon Jesus. A verse that came to mind at that time was Psalm 141:8. "But my eyes are fixed on you, O Sovereign Lord; in you I take refuge do not give me over to death." We prayed fervently that Laura would not be given over to death.

My next question was, "When can we get this tumor out of Laura's brain?" The neurologist said that because the tumor was inter-twined with the speech and logic parts of the brain, it would kill her if they attempted to remove it. This was not something either of us wanted to hear! We asked the doctor if he was absolutely sure that it couldn't be removed. He said he was sure. "What about taking some of it out?", we asked. This is called "debulking". It is done for tumors that are located in such a way that only a percentage can be removed. The doctor again said that there was no way to remove any part of Laura's tumor. He stated that attempting such a surgery would leave her in a vegetative state for the rest of her life. In essence, she would be brain dead.

Anyone who has ever had to deal with cancer knows the biggest, hardest, most troublesome question of all to ask! How long with Laura live? The neurologist said that she would have to have surgery to determine the grade of the tumor before he could definitively tell us the prognosis. He then went on to explain that the shape, size and type of tumor that Laura had typically starts as a grade III or IV.. With this knowledge, the doctor said that Laura had 3 to 6 months and maybe up to 1 year, if they could start treatment right away. This news made us both weep. I have never felt such emotional pain like that before. Unfortunately, I would have to feel this kind of pain many more times in the future. Since I have brought up the grades of tumors, let me quickly try to explain how that works. A specialist must look at part of a tumor to determine what the grade is. Basically, the slower the cell growth, the lower the grade.. Grade I tumor cells are grow very slowly. In many cases, a Grade I tumor won't cause problems for many years. Depending on the type of cancer, people can even live a full life with a grade I tumor. A Grade II tumor is a little more serious, but still has a fairly slow growth rate. With a grade III tumor, the specialist can actually see the cancer cells splitting while they are looking at them under the microscope. Grade IV is the worst. In a grade IV tumor, the cells are very rapidly dividing at a rate that is really hard to slow down. The neurologist told us that Laura needed to be set up for a brain biopsy so that he could get a definitive diagnosis, and a definitive grade on the tumor. The appointment was set up for the following week.

Before leaving the neurologist's office that day, he handed another hard hitting blow to the both of us. At this time, Laura was 5 months pregnant. The neurologist told her that if she wanted to live another six months or more, she would have to abort our child. The doctor made it sound as though Laura had to abort the baby, so we "Almost" lost our second child. He said that there was no way they could do radiation, chemo, or give her certain medications while she was pregnant. Laura knew exactly where I stood on abortion, and she had the same stance. So Laura verified with the doctor that she had at least 3 months to live if she went without treatment. Laura then made the suggestion to continue the pregnancy three more months, and then deliver the baby prematurely, at the 8 month mark. The doctor said that it could be done, but he cautioned against it. But Laura could not justify taking the life of someone that had an opportunity to have a full life, when she was told she only had a maximum of one year to live. The doctor was hesitant, however, because he said he is obligated to treat the patient - not something that "is not a living being yet". It makes me sad when people don't recognize unborn children as living beings with value and worth! Laura placed so much worth in this child that she was willing to give up a portion of her life for it. This was like witnessing a very small glimpse of what Christ did for me. Jesus came to die on a cross for you and me, even though we weren't born yet! I remember praying for this doctor at a later time, that he would come to Christ, and see life as Christ sees it.

From the neurologist's office, I drove us over to my parents' house. We were in shock from what we had just been told by the doctor. Now we had to tell our loved ones the news as well. It's very therapeutic to talk with others about the grief you face. In a small way, it feels like they can take a fraction of it upon themselves. The weight that I felt on my chest that day made me think I was going to have a heart attack. My soul hurt so deep inside. I saw the confusion and hurt in my wife's eyes. I wanted so desperately to take this pain from her. I even asked God to take it from her and give it to me instead. I would be lying if I said I didn't blame God a little for what was happening. Thank you Jesus for having big enough shoulders to hear my cries of anger as well as my praises! My parents consoled us the best they could. It's good to have strong Christian parents who try to see the positive sides of bad situations. They encouraged us by saying that everything would be alright. God would see us through this trying time. God seems to bring me back to the book of Job whenever my life has been hard. I guess just when I think I have it bad, it's comforting to know that some people have had it worse! Job 5:6-9 says, "For hardship does not spring from the soil, nor does trouble sprout from the ground. 7 Yet man is born to trouble as surely as sparks fly upward. 8 But if it were I, I would appeal to God; I would lay my cause before him. 9 He performs wonders that cannot be fathomed, miracles that cannot be counted." It was definitely a hard time in our lives. We sure needed God to perform miracles..

Due to the brain cancer diagnosis, the doctor wrote a letter explaining that Laura would never be able to return to work again. Most people say that they wish they didn't have to go to work. But if they were told they couldn't work anymore, they might feel different. We really take a lot of things for granted, and we complain about many things in life that others would love to have the ability to participate in.. It was hard to deliver this letter to work on Laura's behalf. She couldn't bring herself to do it in person. My wife and I carried the largest case loads in the office.. We both went back and forth each week at the top adjuster's position for claims taken per day. We were both taking around 8.6 claims per day, and the nearest to either of us was 6 claims per day. Instead of dispersing Laura's case load out to everyone, I asked that it all be given to me to work. So along with everything else that was going on, I took on twice the work load. I'm so thankful that Laura worked for a company that had short term and long term disability insurance. Without it, out we wouldn't have made it. Laura went on short term disability for 6 months until long term disability kicked in. Then after a year, Social Security picked up the majority, and what they didn't cover, long term disability did. I found myself more immersed in my work than before. People at work asked me how I could do so much, and keep going with what was happening at home. I found that the harder I worked, the easier it was to forget about the problems at home. Essentially, I was trying to run away from this troubling time.

The day of the biopsy finally arrived. It was so terrifying to know that someone was going to go into my wife's brain, and pull a small piece of it out. Of course, the hospital always makes you sign your life away beforehand.

They say that the risk is minimal, but there is always a chance of paralysis or death with any brain procedure. That didn't do a lot of good for my nerves. It's like the pharmaceutical commercials you see on television. With all of the side effects that they disclose, I have to say I would rather just stick with whatever the problem is in most cases, rather than create new problems by taking the drug.

Laura's biopsy was performed by first using the MRI scan to determine where to enter the brain. A metal halo contraption was then bolted to Laura's head. Yep you read it right the first time - they bolt this thing to the head. If you get sick easily, skip this part! Next, four shots are administered - two in the back of the head, and two in the forehead. These shots numb the area for the drilling in of the bolts. Once the numbing agent has had time to work, the metal halo can be bolted into the skull with a drill. Unfortunately, the numbness only offered minimal relief to Laura, who could still feel the tearing and pressure of the bolts going into her skull. The burning smell of her skin and bone was not delightful either. If you just read that, and you're not feeling well, hey, I put a disclaimer in beforehand! Once the metal halo was affixed to Laura's head, they wheeled her off into an operating room where I was unable to follow and witness the procedure first hand. However, the doctor explained to me what happened next.. Once in the operating room, they drilled a small hole in the skull. Then they guided a small camera/cutting tool through the hole, to the area of the brain that they wanted to biopsy. Once they saw what they wanted, they cut a small piece of tissue from the brain. The brain tissue was then put in a vile and sent off to pathology, where the grade of the tumor would be determined.. I was also informed that the grading process isn't an exact science, as different parts of a tumor can have different grades. Something else that I learned during this process, is that the brain doesn't feel pain. Therefore, the shots that were given were meant only to numb the skin around the skull due to the nerve ending there. The brain itself has no nerve endings. You can poke it all you want and have no pain. However, while it may not hurt, poking the brain can cause a loss of function in a specific area of your body, depending on which part of the brain you damage. I thought that was fascinating and weird at the same time. As we went through this process, I reflected on 1 Corinthians 12:21-22. "The eye cannot say to the hand, 'I don't need you!' And the head cannot say to the feet, 'I don't need you!' 22 On the contrary, those parts of the body that seem to be weaker are indispensable." This verse really hit home. The head is the control center, and it was getting weaker. However the brain is indispensable and life doesn't exist without it.

A long week went by while we waited for the biopsy results. We were both praying hard that the tumor was only a Grade I or Grade II. Waiting is one of the hardest things to do in life. That's probably why the Bible speaks so much about having patience. In James 5:7-11 it says, "Be patient, then, brothers, until the Lord's coming. See how the farmer waits for the land to yield its valuable crop and how patient he is for the autumn and spring rains. 8 You too, be patient and stand firm, because the Lord's coming is near. 9 Don't grumble against each other, brothers, or you will be judged. The Judge is standing at the door! 10 Brothers, as an example of patience in the face of suffering, take the prophets who spoke in the name of the

Lord. 11 As you know, we consider blessed those who have persevered." You have heard of Job's perseverance and have seen what the Lord finally brought about. The Lord is full of compassion and mercy. Oh how He has been teaching me more and more patience through this "Almost" ten year journey. I used to be a much more anxious person before Laura's cancer. Although I would much rather have remained impatient and anxious and had a healthy wife, than to be taught patience through this strenuous ordeal! A week finally went by, and it was back to the neurologist for the results of the biopsy. The verdict was in - it was classified as a Grade III tumor. We were so hurt that it wasn't a lower grade, but at the same time, we were happy it wasn't a grade IV, which would have been the worst news.

We knew exactly what we were fighting now. That was good and bad. The internet today has such a wealth of information.. This information can be scary when you're doing research on a cancer diagnosis! I spent hours upon hours researching the type of cancer Laura had. The more research I did, the more scared I got. However, my searching did reveal that if Laura could have any of the tumor taken out, the radiation and chemo to work more effectively. The research also stated that radiation and chemo should be started immediately. Well that wasn't an option due to Laura being pregnant. I also read that if Laura couldn't have a portion of the tumor taken out, that her life span would at best be 1 year. People that have had some of it taken out typically lived 3 to 5 years. Everything was on a big bell curve. No matter what number I saw, it was terrifying. My wife was 30 years old at the time, and was given a death sentence. I have read countless survivor stories from people that have had the same diagnosis as Laura. In those readings, I determined that the longest any person has lived with this type of cancer is 10 years and two weeks. I did the best that I could to follow these people's stories as they were updated on the cancer survivor websites. The last updated post from the people I was tracking was from 5 years ago. I hope that some of these people are still fighting today, and that they just didn't have time to update their posts. By the way, at the end of this book I will give you my e-mail address. If you're battling brain cancer, and have questions or need to be held up in prayer, feel free to write me. It's important that I tell you some of to Laura's history, so you can understand where some of our fear was coming from. Laura is the oldest of two. She has a sister six years younger than her. When Laura was just 12 years old, her mother was diagnosed with lung cancer. The cancer was very aggressive and soon went to the brain. Within six months Laura's mother passed away. At that time, Laura's dad didn't want to take care of his kids, so Laura's maternal grandparents stepped in to raise them. Now that Laura had cancer, she was so fearful that history was repeating itself. She did not want to pass away at a young age and leave two children behind as well. I encouraged my wife to start writing everything down in a journal. She took my advice and began to write down what she was feeling, and things that she wanted our three year old and unborn child to know. Every once in a while, I would pick up the journal and read it. It would make me weep. Oh how the tears would flow down my cheeks. I would think, "Surely God, you will heal Laura. Surely Lord, you will give her a long life with her children!" The grieving process starts as soon as a loved one is diagnosed with cancer. When one person has cancer, it is like the whole family has cancer. Each person must deal with loss in their life. If you know someone who is battling cancer, please don't forget to pray for their spouse and family as well!

Back at work, I thought I was doing well and handling everything just fine. After all, I'm a strong man, I can handle anything! Famous last words! I was working hard and grieving at home. It didn't seem like I could get any rest in my life. My world was upside down, and it was affecting my health in a negative way. I was going into big time depression. I would sit in front of my television, and eat a ½ gallon of ice cream all at once. I was gaining weight fast. I took on an attitude of not caring much about anything. I remember feeling very numb to the world around me. One day at work, my supervisor was telling me that she was feeling depressed, and wanted to end her life. I responded, "Yeah, I want to go home and stick my gun in my mouth to end it all as well." I really didn't want to blow my head off, but I was crying out for help! "I can't handle the situation that I'm in. I'm way over my head here! Does anyone care about the hurt that I'm going through?" Well the supervisor went to the boss above her, telling him what I had said. She forgot to mention that she wanted to end her life as well. It must have slipped her mind. I was called into the office immediately, and told that while my job was not in jeopardy, they were going to give me time off to go see a doctor. My employer was understanding, and treated me more than fairly. I went up to Los Angeles to see the company doctor. He gave me a test that consisted of about 500 questions. Then he met with me. He told me I was clinically depressed and need to be on anti-depressants. I don't think I needed a 500 question test to figure that out though! I was prescribed

Paxil to help balance out my mood. I also had to meet with someone in San Diego 3 times per week for 2 weeks, until they were sure I wasn't suicidal, and then I was cleared to go back to work. Dear reader, in no way do I advocate the use of medication for all circumstances. However, if you're in a hard grieving situation, there is no shame in getting help and talking to a professional. If medication is determined to be needed, then it's alright. If you're not mentally well, you can't be there for the people that really need you.

In the meantime, we had to wait for 3 months for our second child, Jakob, to be viable enough to be born. We couldn't just sit around and do nothing. We were told by several people that we should opinions from other neurologists. Perhaps we could find one that would be willing to take part of the tumor out. Doctors are human and they can make errors. We have also come to find out that some of them care less about the people they are treating than they should. In order to get other opinions, we needed copies of Laura's MRI scans. It was expensive to get several copies, but we paid for them. Then I learned about "tumor boards". These boards are made up of some of the brightest neurologists, and neurosurgeons in the world. We decided to send Laura's MRI scans off to a few of them in hopes of receiving some other opinions. Sometime later, we received word back from both Harvard Medical and Boston Medical, indicating that the original diagnosis was accurate and that nothing that could be done. However, we then got news from a neurosurgeon from UCLA, who believed he could remove up to 30% of the tumor. He stated that if he took 30% of it out, it would give Laura up to a 5 year life span instead of just one year at best. When you're 30 years old with a three year old and a baby on the way, you are willing to try anything to extend life. We made an appointment with this neurosurgeon, and met with him in Los Angeles. He explained everything to us very simply. With any brain surgery, he said, there are a lot of risks. Due to the location of Laura's tumor, he calculated a 50% chance that she could be left without the ability to talk, as well as a 50% chance that she could die. He asked Laura if she was willing to accept the 50% odds that it may kill her. Laura, who is a true optimist every second of the day, immediately responded that she would be on the good side of 50%, so she could do it, no problem. The neurosurgeon said that he would have to wait for at least one week after the birth of our child before he could operate on her. He was confident he could help Laura, so we left his office very excited for at least a little good news. Just before we left, he said that it would up to us to get prior approval from the medical provider to do the surgery. We said to each other, "No problem, that can't be that difficult to do!"

The healthcare insurance system is a nightmare to deal with!!!! Here we had a doctor that said he was confident that he could help Laura live for up to 4 years longer. Surely the insurance company would gladly pay to extend someone's life right? It's hard for me to tell you this, but the healthcare system is more concerned about the dollar cost associated with a surgery then they are about any individual life. Unless you're someone of importance by the world's standards, then you're just a number. Our insurance company had received a letter from the neurologist that made the initial diagnosis. He stated no surgery could be done whatsoever. The insurance company then got a letter from the neurosurgeon that stated he could take up to 30% of it out, and extend her life. The insurance company decided to take the side of the first doctor, and denied us coverage for this surgery. They actually told us we were denied, because the cost outweighed the benefit! It's sad that the healthcare system sees dollar signs instead of extended life. Laura and I were stressed out to the max by now. We had paid for MRI scans. We sent them all over the place. We found a doctor that was confident he could help us. We sent letters urging the insurance company to reconsider. Even today with any of Laura's treatments, it's a constant fight with the insurance carrier. When people are going through traumatic times in their lives, they shouldn't have the added burden of how a surgery can be covered.

Prayer, prayer and more prayer is all we could rely on. When life has you on your knees, then you're in the right position to go to God with your pain and hurt. My church in San Diego was always loving and supportive through this whole ordeal. I knew that big time prayer warriors were lifting Laura up on a constant basis. Well, God answered those prayers. My friend and former boss Lawrence, who I worked for in the gas station business, was willing to pay for the surgery up front. The surgery was going to cost around one million dollars. Lawrence had his attorney send a letter to the insurance carrier, advising them that he would pay for the surgery. However, he added that if Laura lived over the 1 year mark, then he would go after them for malpractice, and stand to lose many times the amount of the cost of the surgery. The insurance company must have read the attorney's letter, and looked at my friend's bank account. We received a letter one week later, telling us they would cover the surgery after all. Dear reader, if you ever have to go toe to toe with the insurance company, don't back down. My wife was worth the fight. If Laura and I would have just rolled over and played dead, then my wife would not be here today! Thank you, Jesus, for putting a friend like Lawrence into our lives at just the right moment. God answers prayers in very mysterious ways. I have seen so many prayers answered on this journey, and I will share some even bigger answered prayers with you as we continue..

Laura made an appointment with her OBGYN to check on the health of the baby. Also, since Laura couldn't have chemo or radiation, the doctor had to decide what levels of seizure and steroid medications she could take without harming the baby. The steroids were needed to reduce the swelling in the brain. Every week, Laura had to have her blood tested, to make sure the medication levels were in check and not adversely affecting the baby. When Laura was about 8 months pregnant it was determined that the baby was healthy enough to be taken early. The c-section was scheduled for Tuesday, March 13th, 2001, at 11a.m. Now that this date was set, we were able to schedule Laura's brain surgery for Monday, March 19th, 2001 at 8a.m. It was now time to wait again!

March 13th had finally arrived! Both Laura and I were very nervous. We knew that anytime a baby is delivered early, there can be complications. Also, due to Laura's brain cancer, any surgery put her at great risk. We both prayed together before she was wheeled back to the operating room. We asked the Lord to be with the surgeons and to watch over our new baby.. Lastly, we asked the Lord to be with Laura, and to give her the strength to make it through this procedure. I gave my wife a kiss, and off she went to deliver the baby. Due to Laura's cancer, we decided that she would also have her tubes tied while they performed the c-section. I went to the waiting room where most of my family was at waiting as well. It was eerily quiet.. Finally at 12:30 p.m., a nurse came in to notify me that at 12:19 p.m., they successfully delivered my son, Jakob Lee Presley, 5lbs 6oz and 18 inches long. Jakob was taken to the Neonatal Intensive Care Unit. I was told that his lungs were not fully formed, and that they needed to keep a close watch on him, and assist him in his breathing. The nurse said the first week would be the roughest, and if we got past that he would be fine. Because of the wires and tubes that Jakob was hooked up to, we weren't allowed to hold him for the first week. However, Laura was permitted to hold him after just 4 days, since she would be leaving to have her brain surgery soon. Jakob started to feed on a bottle after only 8 days. During that time, I was able to come into the neonatal unit to hold and feed him. Jakob ended up being just fine. He is a little fighter with the same personality as my wife. God knew that Jakob would need that extra spunky personality to make it. Oh boy does he have a spunky personality! Thank you Jesus for a wonderful healthy baby! Laura and I were filled with such joy, and felt blessed to have Jakob in our lives. Laura spent a total of 2 days in the hospital. The only place that kicks you out faster than a hospital is jail! Jakob would spend a total of two weeks before he was able to come home.

Now that the one big surgery was over, we were anticipating the really big one in a week's time. We wanted time to slow down. Neither one of us was looking forward to the following Tuesday. I knew there was a 50% chance that I would "Almost" lose my wife to brain surgery. The week we had together before the surgery was filled with tension. Neither of us really wanted to speak of what could possibly happen. However, no matter how painful it was we both knew we needed to discuss those possibilities. Laura told me about her hopes and dreams for the two kids. She asked me to make sure both Kaleb and Jakob knew all the time that she loved them very much. Laura would sob heavily as she would tell me the things she wanted her children to know. She would tell me to make sure they knew that she didn't purposely leave them, that she didn't choose to get sick, and that she loved them both very much. We both spent a lot of time that week crying, and holding onto each other. I was as supportive and understanding as one can possibly be without going through it myself. It was such a tough week.

The Sunday before the big surgery was such a blessing to the both of us. The senior pastor made an announcement from the pulpit that Sunday morning. He said that Laura was having major brain surgery on Tuesday. He stated that there was going to be a prayer time for Laura and our family following the second service and that anyone who wished to come was invited. It was a nice gesture from the senior pastor, but I thought that people had enough to worry about in their own lives, or would just be too busy to come and pray over my wife. We were both blown away at what happened after the second service. I don't believe anyone at the church left that day. I didn't take a head count, but it looked like a thousand people packed into the upper building of the church. Laura and I were in the middle, sitting down. We had people all around us touching us. 2 Timothy 1:6 says, "For this reason I remind you to fan into flame the gift of God, which is in you through the laying on of my hands." Psalm 23:5 says, "You prepare a table before me in the presence of my enemies. You anoint my head with oil; my cup overflows." These God fearing people were following scripture by laying hands on us, and oil was placed on both of our heads. This was no ordinary prayer meeting lasting only ten minutes or so. People were praying without ceasing for close to 4 hours. We all felt that God was truly with us. It felt like an upper room experience. I have never felt such love from Christ followers since that day. Oh the miracles that happen when people that love the Lord are willing to gather in fervent prayer! I honestly don't believe anyone there knew how much time had really passed, because the spirit of the living God was falling afresh on everyone. Time seemed to stand still. James 2:17 says, "In the same way, faith by itself, if it is not accompanied by action, is dead." It takes very little action on the part of a believer to simply say that they will pray for someone. Be a person of God that actively lives out your faith. Oh church, be willing to wrap your arms around the sick and the hurting. Don't just say you're going to do something, take action. Christ didn't just say "I'm going to the cross to die for you and me." He proved his love for the church by sacrificially giving up his life, so that we now have the opportunity through faith in him to be saved ourselves. Matthew 18:20 says, "For where two or three come together in my name, there am I with them." That tells me that the Lord wants believers to put their faith into practice. If we have two or three believers present, He is there with us. Well, we had plenty more than three people at that prayer meeting. The

Lord still hears the cries of his people.

Just a few hours after the powerful prayer time at church, it was time for Laura to head to Los Angeles for brain surgery the next morning. Since our new born baby Jakob was still in Neonatal intensive care, we both agreed that I would stay behind in San Diego to look after him. My wife's father and step mom came to pick Laura up from my house to take her to Los Angeles. The final ten minutes before Laura got into the car to leave was so emotional. I knew that the neurosurgeon gave Laura a 50% chance to survive the surgery. In my mind, a 50% chance was a coin flip. I really didn't like those odds! I know that we had just finished praying for her in a mighty way, but in the back of my mind I still had worries. At this time I had a newborn and a 4 year old. I couldn't help but wonder how I was going to raise my two boys if their mother didn't come back.. Matthew 6:27 says, "Who of you by worrying can add a single hour to his life?" I knew full well that God didn't want me to worrying. He wanted me to trust completely in him that Laura was in His hands. I sure wish it was that easy. I have to be honest, and tell you that I was terrified at the thought of losing my wife. The angst I felt inside was not peaceful at all. Another verse that popped in my head during this time was Matthew 17:20. It says, "He replied, 'I tell you the truth, if you have faith as small as mustard seed, you can say to this mountain "Move from here to there" and it will move.'" Nothing will be impossible for you. Well I'm guessing that because the mountains are not moving all that much, that you and I don't have that kind of faith. It's not that we don't want to have it. I just think in our imperfect body, it's not possible to have faith that strong! I held Laura in a long loving embrace. We wept many tears in those few minutes. I was scared and thought I would surely lose my wife to this surgery. The doctor also told us that if Laura survived the surgery, it was likely she wouldn't be able to speak again. So I was not only worried about her dying, but that if she lived I wouldn't hear her voice again. We looked into each other's eyes one last time before she got into the car. Laura was stronger at that moment than I was. She reassured me that everything would be fine. If it weren't for her strength and resolve, I would have never made it through! Surely the Lord was with my wife giving her a peace above all understanding!

Well I didn't sleep well that night. My wife was by herself, and I couldn't be there to comfort her. The next morning around the scheduled start of her surgery, I got down on my knees, and prayed! "Lord, be with my wife, and hold her hand the entire time. Lord, be in the room with the doctors and Laura. Lord, give them wisdom that can only come from the almighty healer. Even though I was praying hard, it was difficult to keep my mind and body from being anxious. I was checking my watch constantly. Time seemed to go into ultra slow motion.

The plan was to have one surgery on Monday morning, and then a second bigger surgery on Tuesday. The Monday surgery was to be a short 1 hour procedure. Laura would have to be awake for this one, so that she could talk while the doctors pinpointed the logic and speech area of her brain. This type of procedure is called electronic mapping. Basically, the doctors poke certain areas of the brain while the patient counts. The electronic mapping of Laura's brain would determine the precise points where the doctors would make their cuts during the actual surgery the next day. This is what would allow the neurosurgeon to get up to 30% of the tumor out. All of this was explained to the both of us long before this day was upon us. Having a pretty good idea of what was being done, I was anticipating a phone call from Laura's dad an hour after the surgery had begun. When I didn't receive a call after two hours, I was getting frantic! Shortly thereafter, however, the phone rang. It was Laura's dad, and he told me that the news was not good.. He said that when the neurosurgeon opened her skull to do the electronic mapping, the pressure was so great inside Laura's head, that the tumor pushed through the skull. The Dr. had to quickly put Laura under, since she was supposed to be awake for this first part. A nurse came out to inform her Dad that they couldn't do the electronic mapping, and were going straight into surgery. Without the electronic mapping, the nurse informed him, they would only be able to remove 10% of the tumor. Furthermore, the pressure that was in Laura's brain decreased her chances of survival. All my fingernails were already chewed down to the nubs by that time. Another 5 grueling hours went by, waiting for any word back on Laura's surgery. Finally, I received some news. It was miraculous. The Neurosurgeon said that he was easily able to distinguish the good tissue from the bad tissue with his naked eye. This was the first miracle, because that's just not something that can usually done, and is why they normally require electronic mapping. Furthermore, the neurosurgeon explained that he felt compelled to cut more than what his rationale told him to. Feeling as though he didn't have any alternative, this doctor was able to remove 80% of the tumor! This was nothing less than a miracle that just took place. With technology, the doctor thought he could get up to 30%of the tumor. Once technology was out the door, they thought 10% would be a good result. Well, nothing is too big for the Lord. I believe He orchestrated the whole thing to show that this wasn't the doing of a skilled surgeon, but the divine intervention of a powerful living God! The many prayers for miracles and healing became a reality. Praise God for his mighty hand! Lord, thank you for intervening on Laura's behalf. Thank you, Lord for letting me witness a miracle firsthand! After her surgery, it was off to the Intensive Care Unit for Laura to do some healing.

Laura's Dad would call me frequently to give me updates on her condition. He said she was very sore. Her head and face were very swollen. She was black and blue over her entire face. Her Dad said it was hard to recognize her the day after the surgery. Laura was kept very medicated for the high level of pain she was in.. The doctor told us we were not out of the woods yet. If Laura could get through the next 48 critical hours, her chance of survival would go up. The doctor put a hole in Laura's head to allow the brain to release pressure caused by swelling. Just like any person who has a major brain injury, the swelling inside the brain is the most dangerous. The chances of getting a clot or a stroke are always high following this type of surgery. One of the ways to try to keep the blood from clotting is to put air boots on the legs. So on both of Laura's legs were these boots that would periodically fill up with air. It put pressure on the legs kind of like a blood pressure cuff. This pressure forced the blood out of her legs, and back up into her body. These boots were essential to decrease the likelihood of getting clots. This was critical for Laura, since she couldn't take anti clotting drugs, , because if her blood was to thin, she would bleed out in her brain. The Lord continued to heal Laura's head. She made it through the critical time period without any complications. Remember me telling you earlier that the only place that kicks you out faster than a hospital is jail? Well after only 3 days post brain surgery, the doctor said she could go home. We all thought this was way too soon to be letting her go home after such a major surgery! But back home she came. I was so excited and overjoyed to hold my wife in my arms again! It was like getting a gift at Christmas time! Her face was still black and blue. Her head was still swollen. I wondered if the swelling was normal. But Laura's dad said, "You think that's swollen? It was 4 times worse than that the day after surgery!" I couldn't imagine what that would have looked like.

While Laura was away in the hospital, Jakob became strong enough to leave the hospital as well. Having my wife and child fighting for their lives in a hospital at the same time was difficult. That Thursday, Laura was at our apartment in North Park to recuperate. She was now able to hold Jakob in her arms, and feed him. Oh the joy that filled my heart to see Laura enjoy our new born baby. Laura was excited of course to hold Kaleb, and give him love as well. "Almost" losing one's life and the life of your baby puts a different perspective on life! God was sure teaching me patience the hard way. Laura still didn't have a lot of strength that day. She stayed awake as long as she possibly could to gaze into the eyes of Jakob. It was a hallmark moment to say the least. Mom and her children in loving embraces! Dear reader, I want to give you a challenge, if you have children of your own. We had always done this before,, but it became even more prevalent in our lives after this ordeal. We tell each of our kids we love them, very often. Sometimes so much so that our kids will say, "Ah Dad, (or "Ah Mom"), I know that." Even some don't believe that our kids ever get tired of being told how much they're loved. I also don't believe that there is an age in where your kids don't want to hear it. Life is so precious and short on this side of eternity. We need to make sure our kids and loved ones know they are loved. Our Heavenly Father loves us so much, that he demonstrated it with the ultimate cost on the cross. John 3:16 says, "For God so loved the world that he gave his one and only Son, that whoever believes in him shall not perish but have eternal life." That's some amazing love for you and me! I challenge you right now to put this book down for a moment. Go to your kids, or if needed, pick up the phone. Tell them you love them so very much! It never gets old to hear that you're loved. It will make your child's day, and it will make your heart happy as well.

The next morning, Laura got up early with me. Kaleb was attending pre-school at the time at my church. Laura said she felt like she had enough energy to go with me to take Kaleb to school. I thought it was a little too early for her to be up and about. Trust me, if you know Laura, when she makes up her mind about something, there's no stopping her! I just think she felt like she was missing out on a lot of stuff with the kids. And its hard to tell mom "no" when it comes to her children! Kaleb's pre-school was only 10 miles away. It was supposed to be a quick trip over to drop him off, and then back home again. Laura didn't experience any problems on the way to drop Kaleb off. After checking Kaleb into school, and giving him a million hugs and kisses, we were off to get Laura back home. As I turned out of the parking lot, things got scary. Laura started to have a lot of trouble breathing. She was gasping for air! She also said that her chest was killing her. She said it felt like a ton of bricks were on her chest. My first thought was she was having a heart attack. Change of plans in a hurry. I called my parents to let them know what was happening. I asked if I could drop Jakob off with them so that I could take Laura into the emergency room. My parents have always been there for us through these tough times. I dropped Jakob off and took Laura to the hospital. Laura was not doing well at all. By the time we got to the hospital her struggle to breathe was even worse. I was so scared. I thought for sure this was a complication from the brain surgery, and that I would "Almost" lose my wife to cancer again!

When I brought her into the emergency room, I saw a nurse at the front desk. I told her that my wife is having an immense amount of pain in her chest and is having trouble breathing. The nurse asked if there was any history of heart problems. I responded, "No, but she just had major brain surgery less than a week ago, does that count?" Well that got the nurses attention! I had been to the emergency room several times in the past, and had to wait forever for Laura to be seen. As soon as I said "brain surgery last week", they flew into action. Another nurse came running over with a wheel chair, and Laura sat down. Into a room we went very quickly to start running tests. One of the test they did right off the bat was to see what her oxygen saturation levels were.. I saw the worried looks on the nurse's face when the Oxygen level registered extremely low, at only 40%. Laura was barely getting enough oxygen to remain conscious. The nurse put a mask over Laura's mouth, and started an oxygen flow. They wanted Laura to lie down, but when she did that the pain and breathing became even worse, so she was allowed to stay in the sitting position. A doctor came into the room about 10 minutes into this ordeal. I'm sure he had a good idea what was going on, but wanted to get an x-ray of Laura's lungs first. Laura was taken away in her hospital bed to get the needed scans of her lungs. On this day, the process was remarkably quick. Within 20 minutes they wheeled her back to the room where I was waiting. About a half an hour later, another doctor asked me to walk with him down the hall, because he needed to speak with me. I was immediately concerned, and so was Laura. What did he have to say to me that he couldn't say to Laura? He told me that he didn't want to scare Laura (but I guess it's alright to scare the spouse?). He stated that Laura had thrown 20 (you read it correctly, 20!) pulmonary embolisms through her heart and into her lungs. One pulmonary embolism has an over 90% chance of being fatal, and my wife had 20 of them. The doctor Said, "I'm sorry Mr. Presley, there's nothing that we can do for her." He stated they would keep her medicated for the pain, but that she would die in the next few hours! I was about to "Almost" lose my wife again!

I felt so scared and alone at that moment in the hospital. I had been on an emotional roller coaster over, and over again for the last 3 months. I didn't want Laura to see me get emotional, so I went outside. I was sobbing, and shaking my fist at God. I said, "God you got her through delivering our second child Jakob. God, you were there in the operating room with the surgeon, and performed a mighty miracle with her brain surgery. God, why all of this just to "Almost" a week later take it all away from me?" I was being selfish then. I didn't say that to myself at the time, but looking back, I was more worried about poor Dale then I was about my wife. I had masked my selfishness in prayer for my wife. What I was really telling God was, "You can't take Laura right now. I can't make it on my own. I have two young boys, and I just can't raise them without their mother." I was telling God that I don't do the "going it alone" thing very well. I really needed someone else I could count on to give me support. I'm not proud of the fact that I was more concerned with what would happen to me next, rather than my wife's feelings, and needs at that moment. I've learned that when really trying times come along in a person's life, the fleshly part of who we are can easily creep in. When we start to shake our fist at God, we are too busy yelling to hear Him gently whispering that it will be alright and that we can trust Him! That day and night, I wrestled with so many emotional thoughts. Here I was, 31 years old, dealing with life and death matters! I thought, "I must have really bad luck, because this is not at all what I thought married life was going to be like - especially this early on in life!" It's just impossible to put down every weird emotional thought that was going through my head that day. I hope you can understand though, that this was a spiritual battle.. The following verses are a good reflection of the type of pain I was feeling: Job 6:2-3 says, "If only my anguish could be weighed and all my misery be placed on the scales! 3 It would surely outweigh the sand of the seas no wonder my words have been impetuous."

After composing myself, I would go back in, and spend more time with Laura. I didn't know when her last breath would be, but the doctors assured me it would be soon. Laura knew she was in grave condition, even though I never told her what the doctor had told me. I just felt it would possibly make her panic, and cause her to pass away sooner. She was in so much pain that day, even with the medications they were giving her. I hated seeing her in so much pain. When the physician that had been attending her left for the night, he said, "I'm very sorry for your loss", as he fully expected she would die soon. When he arrived the next morning, he was utterly shocked to find out that Laura was still alive. He then told me that since she has lived this long, we should do something. I was shocked! Why didn't he do something last night, instead of waiting a day to find out she was still alive? Now this doctor had a dilemma on his hands. How would he go about treating her from this point on?

The fact that Laura had been through major brain surgery less than a week prior, was the main obstacle for the medical staff. Normally when someone has a clot, they give them anti-coagulants to break up the clot and thin the blood. But having just had brain surgery, they weren't exactly sure if they could give her these drugs to thin her blood, because it could cause her to bleed into her brain, which would in turn kill her. We were in a situation where if we did something, she could die, and if we did nothing, she could die. I would not have wanted to be in the doctor's shoes that day. I guess that's why they get paid the big bucks! The doctor decided to hold a conference call with the neurosurgeon, and neuro oncologist, in order to come up with the best treatment plan. After that, he had another consent form for me to sign. I had signed so many of these forms to protect the backsides of the doctors, I was used to it by now. He explained that we were in uncharted territory. None of the doctors had any experience with this type of situation, so they were not sure what they wanted to do, or how it would work out. Laura also signed the consent form for further treatment. The doctor then told us that they would be taking her to surgery, to put a green field filter in her body. This procedure called for them to go up her femoral artery, to just below the heart. Once this filter was put into place, it could never be taken out. The doctor believed that the clots actually were being thrown from her abdomen, due to the c-section surgery, and not the brain surgery. Although, they did think that having both surgeries so close together did have some negative effect. Well, that's a "no duh" statement! The filter was meant to keep any more clots from entering her heart, and either giving her a heart attack, or going into the lungs again. This would stop anymore clots from coming from the abdomen, but what about the 20 clots already in her lungs? Well it was explained to us that those clots could break loose at any time and cause more damage. They could travel to the brain and cause a stroke, for example. As it turned out, a couple of the clots actually did make their way into her right arm.. But Laura came through this surgery, once again. God's amazing power coupled with Laura's incredible will to fight kept her living. The doctors were very worried about the next step, however. They injected Laura with a blood thinner called Heparin. After 12 hours, nothing had adversely happened, so they administered another shot to her. A few hours after the second shot, Laura felt the pressure leave from her chest, and her breathing improved. The nurse gave me a crash course on how to administer the Heparin shots to Laura, because she would need them for a week before an oral blood thinner called Coumadin could be taken. The next day, Laura's oxygen level returned to a safe enough level to discharge her. Can you see that God was still teaching me to be patient, and to trust Him in all things? God got Laura and I through another ordeal. Now we were off to pick up Kaleb and Jakob at my parents home, and then get back to our apartment so Laura could recuperate.

The neuro oncologist gave Laura about 2 weeks to recover from the brain surgery, and this latest episode with blood clots, before it was back to a round of radiation and chemo at the same time. If you or someone you know has had to go through chemo or radiation, you will know that they don't make you feel well at all, especially if you get them both at the same time. Laura met with the radiologist that would be administering her radiation treatment. They measured her head, so they could make a special piece of head gear to wear. This head gear would help the radiologist pin point where the radiation was to be concentrated. At this time, a new oral chemo drug came out that had just been approved by the FDA, called Temodar. The people in the clinical trials did very well on this drug. The Dr. said doing both of these treatments at the same time would give Laura a better chance to put the cancer in remission. Laura was told that her hair would all fall out during these treatments. She had long hair, but was never vain about having no hair. Laura would sometimes where a bandana to cover her head, but most of the time she really didn't care what other's thought. I didn't really care either - after all, I didn't fall in love with her hair, but her heart. Going back and forth to radiation every day, five days a week, was a pain, because her strength was being zapped on two ends. The radiation also burned her scalp, and made her feel nauseous. Thankfully, Laura was able to tolerate the chemo drug Temodar when she took it with an anti-nausea medication called Zofran. Medications have come a long ways to keep chemo patients from feeling too sick. The main issue with chemo is that it zaps a lot of the energy out of a person. Most chemo patients end up sleeping a lot.

After six weeks, Laura's radiation was done. Laura remained on chemo for one year, and then we got great news! Laura's cancer was in remission. Praise the Lord! The doctor was more reserved,, however, stating that it was unknown how long it would stay in remission and that it would eventually come out of remission. Additionally, when this type of cancer does come out of remission, it's generally more aggressive than it was before.. The best way to describe remission, is that the cancer cells have merely taken a break from eating up the good brain tissue and spreading. At any rate, at this point we saw this remission as a major victory for Laura! Laura has always had the attitude that this cancer would not defeat her. I believe the Lord has given my wife peace in abundance.

After this first very stressful year was over, we decided to reward each other by going on vacation to Hawaii. We really never had a honeymoon, so it was a well-deserved trip. My parents watched Jakob, while we took Kaleb along with us. It was a good time for both of us to reconnect in our relationship. It seems whenever Laura is sick, it takes a big toll on the quality of our relationship. After a week away, we came back rejuvenated.

About 3 weeks later, we went out to a movie. Later that

night, Laura had a very bad seizure. She had a blank empty stare, and her eyes weren't blinking. I had to take Laura back to the emergency room. With all that had happened in the past year, I thought she might be having a stroke. After an exam, the doctor, told us that Laura's seizure was probably triggered by the movie we saw.. Evidently, the frequency at which the light flickers in a movie theater can trigger a seizure. Since Laura was already on Dilantin, a medication to control seizures, he increased the dosage and added a new medication called Keppra, in an attempt to keep this from occurring again. Unfortunately, that was the last movie Laura and I have been able to go to together. We take so much for granted in life. Something as simple as going to a movie, and we can no longer enjoy this together!

In March of 2003, we decided to move from San Diego to the Phoenix area. A couple of things went into this decision. Laura's grandparents, the ones that helped raise her, lived there. She wanted to be close to them, because she didn't really know how long she had to live. We also wanted to be near Barrow's Cancer Hospital, which was located in Phoenix. I loved San Diego and being close to my family, so the move was tough. But I understood why it was important for Laura to be close to her family during this time as well. It was a sacrifice that I was willing to do for my wife. Right after we got to Arizona, we found the neuro oncologist that Laura is still seeing today.

Laura went through a period of time that was relatively calm. She would continue to have MRI scans every 3 months to make sure the tumor wasn't growing back. The cancer seemed to stay in a holding period until about the fifth year. One of her routine scans showed potential growth, but he neuro oncologist wasn't sure if it was scar tissue, or new growth. As a precautionary measure, Laura was put back on chemo for 6 months. Another MRI scan was taken after 3 months, and the Dr. could see no change to the picture. Then after another 3 months, the scan showed the same thing, so it was determined to be scar tissue, and Laura was off chemo. It's very stressful when a doctor tells you they are unsure whether a tumor is growing or not. I never thought they would put Laura back on chemo, when they didn't even know if it was growing. But nothing shocked me anymore. I became pretty numb to what was going on. I had been up and down the roller coaster so often, that the ride wasn't eliciting a response any longer. In my mind, I was always waiting for the next thing to happen.

After this minor scare at about the fifth year mark, Laura had another long period of time where no major issue arose. We both remembered being so filled with joy that God had sustained her for 5 years. All the doctors stated after her brain surgery that 3-5 years was all she would live. It's always nice when doctors are wrong about bad news.. By the way, if you get nothing else out of this chapter get this: doctors are wrong all the time, God is never wrong! Put your trust in God through the good times and in the times of intense struggle. If God is not done using you yet, then you will not die. If God is done with you in this lifetime, then nothing a doctor does will matter. It's God that determines when you have completed what He needs you to complete, not any one man. Please remember that when you go through your struggles. Take things that are said to you with a grain of salt, and give them to a powerful all knowing God who loves you so much! Your marching orders are from God, and therefore, you must never give up! You might have years, or just days, but God will be using you until you take your very last breath!

Laura continued to do well until we hit the ninth year mark of this journey. One day she drove herself to the grocery store, and called me from the parking lot, asking how to get home. She couldn't remember if she had even paid for her groceries, or why she was there in the first place. She also couldn't remember where she lived, and I had to tell her. I asked her if she needed me to walk over to the store, and get her. We only had one car, so it would have taken me 10 minutes to get to her. I was so worried at this point, because of her state of mind. Laura told me she could make it home. I went outside to wait for her to get home. I was relieved to see her pull into the driveway. When she got out of the car, she could barely walk or talk. It was a real struggle for her to walk down the hall to our bedroom. I told her to go lie down, and I would get all of the groceries taken care of. At that point I thought she was having a seizure again, and was hoping it would get better. After getting the groceries inside, I went back to the bedroom to talk with her. Now she was staring at me, and not talking at all. This seizure was really bad! It took about five minutes to help her back to the car, and then we headed to the emergency room. As soon as I got to the emergency room, I went inside and brought out a wheel chair to bring her in. The nurse at the desk once again started asking questions. I had been through this before, so I said, "Brain cancer patient, possible seizure, or possible stroke." I also briefly explained her other medical issues, like clots in her lungs. They brought her back immediately to be examined.

Now that we were in a room again, a lot of tests were being
performed. Another MRI was taken of her brain, as well as
an EEG. This is a test that measures the brain waves to see
if they are functioning correctly. The doctors were at a loss
for words. They really didn't know what was going on. I
thought that I would again "Almost" lose my wife to
cancer. They said she probably had a horrible seizure, and
she would snap out of it soon. Laura spent about 15 hours
in the emergency room with no progress at all. Her body
shut down, and she couldn't speak. My two boys were 12
years old and 8 years old at this time. They were terrified,
because mom wasn't talking. When the boys were
younger, they didn't understand much. Now I had my two
boys' emotional states to worry about. I would get
questions from them like, "Is mom going to die?" They
would both cry a lot, and say, "We want mom to talk to us.
Why won't she talk to us?" I did my best to assure them
that she would be alright and that her brain just needed a
break right then. My boys and I spent a lot of time praying
that the Lord would heal her again. Due to her condition,
the doctor transferred her into a regular neurology room in
the hospital. After a day of no communication from Laura,
I wasn't sure if she would ever come back to us. I called
family members to let them know what was going on.
Laura's dad drove over right away to be with her in the
hospital. On the third day, she was more alert, but still
couldn't talk. We used a paper and pen to communicate.
At first she had a hard time formulating and spelling words.
It was hard to understand her writing. Sometime on day
four, however, her writing improved. It became tiring to
communicate this way, although I was thankful that at least

she was making progress. After being in the hospital for 7 days, they discharged her. They didn't know whether she would ever regain her speech The next two weeks at home were extremely difficult. My kids would say, "Dad, is mom talking yet? When will she talk?" They would write to her, and draw her pictures that said, "I love you, Mom." They would tell her they wanted to hear her voice again. A person's voice is something else I believe we take for granted until it's not there. I asked God to forgive me for the times I wished Laura would just be quiet. No matter what is being said, hearing my wife talk is important. This was a very trying three week time period. I'm sure it emotionally scarred my two boys. After three weeks, Laura said her first word. To be honest, I don't even remember what the word was, I was just so excited to hear her say something. Her speech fully returned over the next 24 hours. The kids were so elated at hearing their mom speak again. Laura's response about the whole incident was that she just needed to take a break for awhile. My thoughts were, "Will this ever happen again?" Knowing where her cancer is located and what it affects, I know it will eventually happen again. I always wonder what the last words I will ever hear her say will be. When will her speech go away forever? It's really hard to have these thoughts in the back of my mind. Laura and I still have disagreements on things, but I try hard not to. I don't want our last conversation to be something negative.

Laura's neuro oncologist made sure to check in on Laura whenever we were at the hospital. She would tell me that she believed there was more pressure in her brain pushing against the tumor. She also said she saw what appeared to be four tumors in her brain not just one, and this is why she had the latest set back. About a week after she started to walk and talk again, we went back to the hospital to find out what the next step would be. The neuro oncologist suggested that Laura start up chemo again, using the oral drug Temodar. She also prescribed more steroids for any swelling. This Dr. also told Laura that she knew a radiologist that would do a second round of concentrated radiation on these tumors. Normally a person can only have one round of radiation in their lifetime. One round of radiation is equal to the amount of radiation a person would get from the sun if they live for 75 yrs. So you can see it's a great risk to give a person 150 years worth of radiation before they're even 40 years old. Laura never thought twice about it. She said, "The radiation won't harm me, I will do it again." So Laura signed her life away again on a consent form, in order to have a second round of radiation. She went to the radiologist a week prior to the treatment to have them measure her for head gear. Again, this head gear is critical for the radiologist to know exactly where to pinpoint the radiation. Laura made it through this procedure with flying colors. She shaved her head beforehand, because she knew her hair would fall out again. Within a couple of months, most of her hair grew back, except the area where they radiated. The part that did grow back came in curly this time instead of straight. The doctor said that the left part of her head may never grow back, but by about the 5th month, it grew back again as well. My wife has to be getting her batteries charged directly from God, because she just keeps going, and going. The only other side effect from the radiation was that all of her teeth are rotting away. Still today she has a lot of pain in her mouth from her teeth rotting. Unfortunately, with no job and no dental insurance, we can't afford to take care of her teeth at this time. Medical insurance doesn't take care of teeth that are affected by the treatments.

After the radiation was completely done, another MRI scan was taken of Laura's brain. The neuro oncologist stated that the 4 tumors had all shrunk in size, and that the radiation did a great job at reducing them. She did state, however, that her cancer had progressed to a Grade 4, and that she would forever be on chemo. It was further explained to us that she couldn't ever have brain surgery again, or receive a 3rd round of radiation. Chemo was the only way to now manage the tumors inside her brain. Laura was on a constant rotation of the chemo drug Temodar, for 3 weeks on and 1 week off. Laura also started getting an MRI done every 2 months. In May of 2010, the MRI picked up some more growth of the tumors. At that point, we were told about another IV chemo drug called Avastin that had promising results in other brain cancer patients. Avastin is unique in the way it's supposed to work to fight brain cancer. This drug is supposed to go to the cancer cells, and put a bubble around them. When the cancer cell is in this bubble, it can't grow as easily, because it's not getting the nourishment it needs. The problem with Avastin is that it can mask the tumor and keep it from showing up on an MRI scan. I immediately started to do research on this drug. I also have a friend in San Diego that is an RN oncology nurse. I learned from both her and my research that this is a last resort chemo drug. Once a person goes on this, they can never get off of it. Despite was I had learned about Avastin, Laura's physician insisted that she would only need 4 rounds which would take 2 months, and then she would be off of it. I'm not sure if she was actually lying to us, but I do believe that doctors avoid telling patients the whole truth sometimes. I guess it doesn't matter all that much since God's in control, but it would be nice to at least know that you are getting the whole truth from your doctors. Laura still currently takes the chemo drug called Temodar, 3 weeks on and 1 week off. She also goes in every two weeks for an IV treatment of Avastin done.

I have seen my wife lose a lot of weight from being on chemo for so long. She jokes that it's the best weight loss program anyone could ever be on. Her attitude is always a positive one. The chemo also makes her very weak and tired, though. Laura's body needs a lot more rest than usual. She sleeps a lot more. Even so, when the kids are home at night, she still makes a point of helping them out with their homework. We try to have as normal of a family life as possible. I have tried to take over more of the household chores, as well as the cooking. Not being employed for 11 months might have been God's way of saying, "Your job right now is to make sure that your wife and family are being taken care of." Many people have had to point this out to me, because I feel so inadequate not having a job. The numbers of times I've taken Laura to the doctor have been too many to count. I have also spent countless stressful hours on the phone with the insurance companies, who constantly try to deny Laura's chemo medications. Each treatment of chemo costs the insurance company around $1,700.00. In "business land" they care more about the money than the person that needs the medication to survive. It would be a better world if compassion outweighed the almighty dollar.
Unfortunately, sin runs rampant, so that will never be the case. Laura has a great attitude that this cancer will never

get her, but I still feel anxious in my heart. I know God is in control, but it's hard not to worry. I pray that God will need to use Laura in mighty ways for many more years to come. I know that God has already used Laura and me in mighty ways. This book is an example of how God is using Laura's cancer to help others. Only the Lord knows when I will go from "Almost" losing my wife to cancer to having my wife graduate to glory! I must lean and press hard into Jesus for constant strength. If someone you know is going through cancer, please come along side of them. Give them a hug, and let them really know you're with them on this journey. Let God use you to give those people the tangible love that they so desperately need. I encourage you to not only pray for them, but give up your time to show your love to them. I have come to realize that it's easier for people to give a gift, or part with some money in their attempt to show love. But do you know what really makes a difference? Giving up your time to someone. Time is so precious! No price can be put on time. Once it's gone it can't be bought back. If you give up your time to be there in someone else's struggle, they will surely feel loved. Most people don't know what to say to another person that is grieving, so they don't say anything at all. The person going through the struggles and grief knows it's hard for you. No matter what you say, love is what will be conveyed when you give up your time for them! Don't be scared of someone that is ill. They might just be a little closer to getting to glory than you are. However, like my wife always says, I might get hit by a bus tomorrow, and she will outlive me. Live each moment by God's grace, knowing that your next heart beat may be your last, even if you've never been sick a moment in your life.

One of the ways that I'm helping to fight brain cancer is through a company called Rocked Apparel. My brother Brian started the company, and is the president. I'm the vice president of this company. I came up with an idea to have shirts and other items that say " I ROCKED CANCER". We also customize items to replace the "I" with a company's name. For example, "ABC Hardware ROCKED CANCER". For every shirt we sell, we donate $5.00 to brain cancer research. This is important because brain cancer is one of the least funded in terms of research. If you feel so inclined to help out, please visit our website at www.ugotrocked.com.

Thank you for reading through this long chapter about my life. I hope that you or someone you know is able to benefit by what you read. I would like to summarize this chapter by telling you the story in Luke 17:11-19. "Now on his way to Jerusalem, Jesus traveled along the border between Samaria and Galilee. 12 As he was going into a village, ten men who had leprosy met him. They stood at a distance 13 and called out in a loud voice, "Jesus Master, have pity on us!" 14 When he saw them, he said, "Go show yourselves to the priests." And as they went, they were cleansed. 15 One of them, when he saw he was healed, came back, praising God in a loud voice. 16 He threw himself at Jesus' feet and thanked him and he was a Samaritan. 17 Jesus asked, "Were not all ten cleansed? Where are the other nine? 18 Was no one found to return and give praise to God except this foreigner?"19 Then he said to him, "Rise and go; your faith has made you well." There are a couple of things I'd like you to get out of these passages. There were ten men that were sick, and shouted out to Jesus have pity on them. So Jesus took pity on them, and said "Go show yourself to the priests". Back then if a person was sick with leprosy, they had to go to a priest. The priest would examine them. If they were deemed unclean they were quarantined. This meant they couldn't even return to their families. This was probably very stressful for all involved. So when Jesus says "return to the priests" it's so they can examine them. However, the verse says that as they went to the priest's they were healed, so it was the simple step of faith to return to the priests that put into motion the healing process. The sad part is only one of the ten that was healed found the time to find Jesus, and give praise to Him in a loud voice. It doesn't say he was quiet about giving the praise, but he was loud. Why is this important? When God does a miraculous work in your life, don't be timid about it. Shout out to everyone what God has done. Jesus had to ask where the other nine that were healed were. I believe he was asking a rhetorical question. Jesus knew exactly where they were at. Since it says that the foreigner was the one that found Jesus, and gave him praise, I assume that the other nine men were locals. It may have taken much more effort for the foreigner to get back to Jesus then the other nine. Did the locals take what Jesus did for them for granted? Did they just think, "Hey, that's what Jesus does, he heals, and we can go on with our lives?" These ten men each had pain in their life in the form of leprosy. But only one was willing to give praise! Laura and our family have had to endure much pain. I want you to know that I still give praise to God for the healing and miracles that have been done. So reader, when you go through pain, please remember who gets you through it. Don't hold back on being loud for Jesus! My prayer is that all ten people will scramble to find Jesus to give him praise, not just one. Oh how alive our churches today would be if we all gave praise to Jesus for his healing touch in our lives. Dear reader, I challenge you to be a person that is loud and proud of what the Lord is doing in your life, regardless of how hard the journey has been.

Chapter 5 "Almost" had an affair.

Well reader, this is going to be another hard chapter to write. There is so much information that I believe will help you and others out. However, in order to put this information into words, I have to continue to dig up my past sins. In this chapter, I will try to give you an idea of what was happening in my life that would cause me to be vulnerable. I'm not saying that there is ever an excuse to "Almost" have an affair, or to go through with the act itself. I do believe that there are circumstances that we find ourselves in that make it easier for the temptations we face to become a reality! First I think it's important to define what constitutes an affair. What better place to look than the Bible. First, Exodus 20:14 says, "You shall not commit adultery." Mark 10:11-12 states, "Anyone who divorces his wife and marries another woman commits adultery against her. 'And if she divorces her husband and marries another man, she commits adultery'. Matthew 5:27-28 says, "You have heard that it was said, Do not commit adultery. 'But I tell you that anyone who looks at a woman lustfully has already committed adultery with her in his heart'.

Let's go a little deeper into these three passages. Obviously in Exodus 20, it's pretty simple - don't do it, period. In Mark 10:11 says" anyone" who divorces his wife… No one can claim exemption from this passage. Then it says that if I marry another woman I have committed adultery against her. I will talk more about divorce in the next chapter, but for now, if I get divorced, I can't remarry again. If I get married again, it's considered adultery. Now in verse 12, it just says the same thing, but applies it to the wife this time. From what I see so far, God's institute of marriage is air tight. In God's eyes there is but one woman for each man, and one man for each woman. This passage is really hard for me to grasp. Matthew 5:28 says, "I tell you that anyone who looks at a woman lustfully has already committed adultery with her in his heart." Recently I noticed that Jesus didn't say "if a woman looks at a man", but, "if anyone looks at a woman". It's weird how a verse can be read, and something like this can be just glossed over. I will give you my two theories, and maybe I'm off base. First, Jesus did more of his teaching to men than he did to women, so that could explain it. Second, Jesus knew that man was created differently with more of a propensity to be visually stimulated than a woman, so he was warning the man. Again not real sure - just thought it was interesting when I came across it. That verse in Matthew is a real tough one to get around. I understand the whole "get married only one time" thing. But if my eyes wander to lustfully look at another woman, I have committed adultery? Well if you're a man reading this, I hope you're honest with yourself. Has there ever been a time when you looked at a woman, and didn't let your brain just stop at, "Well, she is attractive"? Did your brain take this woman to places it shouldn't have? I'm going to go out on a limb right now, and guess that no man except Jesus Christ has been able to walk on this earth without thinking those types of unwholesome thoughts at least once in their life. Women, you're not off the hook if you've looked at a man with the same thoughts. I often wonder why God made man such visual creatures. So this being said, I have "Almost" had an affair in the common physical sense of the word, but in the biblical sense, there is no "Almost" about it. I have blown it countless times in this area of my life.

I'm finding myself constantly going to God, and asking for forgiveness about how far I let my brain go when I should have stopped it at just my eyes. God made women beautiful to look at period. It should be enough to just marvel at God's creation without being perverted about it. Satan uses God's beautiful creation to try to separate us from Him. I thank Jesus for his continued forgiveness for me in this area of my life.

I believe that if we lustfully look at women with our eyes, and it becomes commonplace, it's not a great leap to the physical act. You see, our brains constantly play tapes over and over in our heads. Thinking only clean thoughts will ensure that the tapes being played in your mind are pure. Unfortunately, this is not always easy. Turn on the television, and impurities are thrown in your face. Have you ever seen a commercial where at the end of it you have to ask what was it that they were selling? I have on several occasions, especially when my eyes were being distracted by actresses in provocative clothing. One way to play better tapes in your mind is to read the Word of God every day. By doing so, you will find yourself thinking purer thoughts, because God's tape is playing in your mind! Reader, if you're a women can I ask you a favor? When you get dressed in the morning, please ask yourself if what you're wearing could be alluring to a man. I'm not telling you by any means what to wear. I am saying that what you wear could cause a man to stumble in his spiritual walk with the Lord. Surely if you're a Christ follower, you wouldn't want that to happen. This may not be the best analogy, but you wouldn't put a beer in front of a recovering alcoholic, would you? Look at it this way – men, whether they want to admit it or not, are recovering sex addicts. This problem in our society is probably worse than most people want to admit. People say that they can handle what they see and that it doesn't affect them. I believe most men cannot take off their masks and be completely honest about how hard it is to keep their mind clean in this area. I will elaborate later in this chapter, but I have struggled with pornography myself. I have taken off my mask in front of my church to come clean to them. Some people in the church embrace the way I was able to show clarity in my struggle with this sin. Others would rather e-mail the pastor to ask why would he would allow someone in church to discuss this matter. I believe the people who sent those emails are still desperately trying to hide behind their masks. If that is the case, then hearing someone with a similar problem confessing their sins publicly might feel like a big screwdriver is being stuck in their back. That's spiritual warfare in the church. If Satan can discourage Christians from openly discussing their sins, he wins! No healing will take place in a church until the church as a whole takes off their masks with each other. Once this happens, everyone will be more concerned about seeking out the lost then hiding behind whatever mask they have put up to cover their sins. You can't hide your sin and seek the lost at the same time!

I believe we all have certain areas of weakness that make us susceptible to temptations. Your areas may be different than mine, but I assure you Satan knows full well what they are. A lot of weaknesses are developed when we are young, and some are born later out of extreme circumstances. If you remember back to chapter one, "Almost" popular growing up, you will find that I have a very low self esteem. This low self esteem didn't appear overnight, it took years to develop. In society today it's getting more difficult to have a good self esteem. People constantly tear others down to make themselves look better. Because of my low self esteem, I have always felt starved for love and attention. Remember back in chapter two, when I resigned from the live-in police academy? I resigned because I wasn't strong enough to be alone without love and attention. If you ever meet me in person, you will probably see that I have a tendency to talk a lot, and be the center of attention. This attention starvation is part of what allowed the "Almost" affair to take place.

When we are at our weakest moments in life, it's so easy to give into temptation. I also believe it's easier to give into temptations with those people we know and trust. We feel more comfortable confiding in those people in hard times. I have several instances where in my pain I tried to get a sense of love from other women. Most of these women were in a strong place in their own life so they weren't easily tempted themselves. Had more of them been in a vulnerable position, I would probably have had more than one "Almost" affair to write about. I will write about some of these instances, as it goes to explaining how easy it is to fall into this trap of lust. Being loved and held can be great, but it can also have such damaging effects!

Let me now introduce to you the woman that I "Almost" had an affair with. To protect this woman's identity I have changed her name and certain other details. This is all about trying to help you recognize the "Almost" moment before it becomes an "Almost" moment in your life. I am going to refer to this woman as "Bertha". You ask why the name Bertha? I asked my wife what name she would like me to use for this person, and she said, "Bertha". I first met Bertha when I was only 15 years old. At that time Bertha was 18 years old, and a senior in high school, while I was in the 10th grade. We met while roller skating. When it was time for the couples skate, I asked her if she would like to skate with me. Reluctantly, she said "yes". She probably just didn't want to hurt a kid's feelings. Well, I wanted that three minute song to last forever. Here was an older, beautiful woman paying attention to me. Not only that, but she holding my hand as we went around the floor. The human touch means so much. I knew that Bertha was there that night with a bunch of her friends. I'm pretty sure I created a good bit of laughter for them. Before that night was over, I was able to garner the courage to ask her for her phone number. To my surprise, she actually gave it to me! You know to this day, I still have the blasted number plastered in my memory bank. The number is no good any longer, but my brain for some reason holds it in high regard.

I'm sure by reading the preceding chapters, you can guess how long I waited to call her. Well, did you guess within 24 hours? Hey you're getting to know me to well by now! I called her up the next night. I was just too excited to wait and play the "hard to get" person. I was thinking that the phone number would not be a good one, so that's part of why I had to call. The other reason was that she didn't have my number, so if she was yearning to call me, she couldn't. I was doing her a favor by not making her wait on me. Yeah I don't really believe that baloney either, but it sounds good! I asked Bertha if she would like to go to a movie with me. The only problem was that I didn't drive yet, so I told Bertha that I would pay for everything if she would pick me up. It felt weird to have a woman pick me up for a date. Anyone else thinking this is obviously not going to go that far? The roller-skating outing was the previous Saturday night, so I had to wait until a week later before our date. It was a wonderful date, but boy was I nervous. Bertha was 3 years more advanced than I in the dating department . I'm sure she was thinking I was naïve when it came to women. Well if she was thinking that, she was absolutely right! At the end of the date, she drove me back home. While sitting out in her vehicle in front of my house, I was very nervous. What's the appropriate way to end this great night? Do I kiss her good night? Do I give her a hug? Do I just say goodnight period? Well, the way I decided to end this date had a lot to do with the fact that my parents kept peeking out the kitchen window at us. They were also concerned how I would choose to end this date. I was angry at the time that they didn't trust me. However, looking back at it, they were right not to trust me. When I leaned over to give Bertha a hug, I could see that she thought a kiss was in order. But since I didn't retreat from the hugging position, a hug was what I got. Please take note of this "Almost" kiss moment - it's going to be very important later in this chapter.

A couple of months went by, and I finally turned sixteen. I had my license and my own car, which I thought would help garner more of her attention. A three year age difference is huge in high school. I did get the opportunity to hang out with Bertha and her friends on a couple of other outings. One of those outings was a bonfire at the beach. Bertha had some friends that were already 21 years old, and they brought wine coolers. My first alcoholic drink was a California wine cooler, orange flavored. Remember, I was not old enough to legally have this beverage. I said "no" to drinks several times before saying "alright" this time. One is all I had by the way, but it was still the wrong thing to do. Never did tell the parents about this one. Well, I guess they'll know now when they read my book. Toward the end of her senior year in high school, she told me that she was accepted to Harvard. She would be leaving after the summer to attend college. That summer went by way too fast. Before Bertha left for college, I gave her a gift to remember me by. I really thought I would never hear from her again. I was certain that once she was with older college men, our chance of ever being a couple was gone. I was actually pretty broken up about the whole thing when she left. To my surprise, about a year later, I received a phone call that she was visiting her parents while she was on a weeklong break from school. We got together, and talked about what was happening in our lives. We were developing a good solid friendship. She told me that she was in a relationship with a guy she liked, and had dated a few times. He was a couple years older than her. I became like the brother she never had. We always felt that we could tell each other anything. Sometimes that's good to have someone close you that you can tell everything too. However, having someone of the opposite sex to confide in can be dangerous, but I will dive into that later. Our friendship has remained strong over the years. Bertha would go on to marry the older guy in college. She now has four girls that keep her busy.

Let me now fast forward to the day my wife received her cancer diagnosis. For you see, that day put into motion a lot of things that strained our marriage. Up until that day, we had minor disagreements, but our love for each other was strong. I had kept in contact with my friend Bertha, but with not much frequency. When two people get married they have a lot of hopes and dreams. One of those is to grow old together. In life, one is born and one must die. However, we assume when we get married that we won't be faced with life or death circumstances until much later on in life. If my wife would have been in her 70's or older when she was diagnosed, I believe my response would have been very different. I was 31 years old, and my wife only 30 years old when this diagnosis came. It was just too darn early to have to deal with what I thought at the time would be the death of my precious wife.

I'm now going to give you a detailed glimpse of what I was thinking and feeling at this time in my life. Again, I don't condone my thoughts or feelings. A lot of it was sinful in nature. In my experience, when life throws me a curve ball I would rather try to work out the situation in my own mind without God. When things were going well I would praise God, but when times were tough, I would retreat from Him. God wants us to be close to Him in our good times and during our trials. Don't turn your face from God. As soon as your face turns, so goes your body. At that point, you lose your proximity to God. Remember that He is the vine, and we are the branches John 15:5. In order for a branch to get nourished, it must abide in the vine. Well, the direction I was headed was not in close proximity to the vine. It's scary to get one's nourishment from what the world has to offer instead of what God wants for us.

Here I was 31 years old, hearing that my wife would die in 3 to 6 months. My wife was pregnant at the time and we had a son aged 3 at the time. I couldn't possibly be all alone, and have to take care of two young boys. I didn't feel strong enough to do it on my own. Being a single parent was not something I thought I would be good at. I needed someone in my life to help me out. My worth was dependent on having another person in my life. In Matthew 19:5-6 it says the following: "For this reason a man will leave his father and mother and be united to his wife, and the two will become one flesh. 6 So they are no longer two, but one." In a sense, God intended me and my wife to become one. So when I thought she would die soon it felt as if my flesh was being ripped apart. I had pain in my heart and soul from this ripping of flesh feeling. I don't know how the soul feels pain, but it was like a ton of bricks on my chest squeezing the life out of my soul. Surely God wouldn't tear my flesh apart by taking my wife at such a young age. Surely God wouldn't leave me to take care of two small children all by myself. Looking back at this now, I know the pain was so great, because my love for my wife was so deep! However, my mind kept taking me places that I really didn't want to go. Oh how the brain can take us on some wild trips!

My wife's sickness would no longer allow her to be as sexually responsive as she was before. I tried to not make my wife feel bad for her inability to satisfy my needs in our marriage. I also know I didn't always succeed in this attempt. I'm sure on several occasions I got mad, and frustrated that sex had taken a back seat to everything. God created sex within the confines of marriage to be beautiful not a dirty thing. It was by God's design to keep the two people together as one flesh. It's so difficult to be one flesh when two married people lose this all important union. One of the verses that stuck out in my head during this time is 1 Corinthians 7:3-5. It says, "The wife's body does not belong to her alone but also to her husband. In the same way, the husband's body does not belong to him alone but also to his wife. Do not deprive each other except by mutual consent and for a time, so that you may devote yourselves to prayer. Then come together again so that Satan will not tempt you because of your lack of self-control". These verses really hit me hard. It doesn't say in these verses that if your wife is ill then all bets are off. It doesn't say that when a partner is sick they can stop fulfilling their marital duty to their partner. It says to not be together for just a little while, and by mutual consent. It says get together again soon, or Satan will have a foot hold in the marriage due to lack of self-control. These are really hard verses to deal with when you're a young married man who would love to be together with his wife. The last part of the verse about Satan getting in the door is also tough. It's no lie! It doesn't seem to matter why the two people can't be faithful, so much as what happens when they aren't. Again, there's no way I blame my wife Laura for her inability to have her body available to me. That being said, I was in desperate need for that piece of the puzzle that was missing in my life.

I didn't want to intentionally hurt my wife. I was just having a horrible time figuring out how to remain true to her, and yet feel the love I had lost. I would even suggest stupid solutions like how about a woman of her choosing to be a substitute. Doesn't even sound right writing it down. I wanted my wife to give me permission to have an affair, but it was purely to take care of the sexual needs, and nothing more. I was saying, "I love you my wife, but since you're out of the game in this area can you help me

131

out?" Of course my wife being very wise would have no part in it. Her response was if you can't handle it, then divorce is the option. I will cover that in more detail in the next chapter. So since I was running out of options to take care of my needs, I turned to the sin of masturbation. Now again my intent is not to scare you off from reading this. I'm trying to be as delicate as possible when I write about this, but I believe some of it is necessary so that you get the full picture. I want you the reader to be inside my thought processes along the way, so that you'll understand my actions. Also, if you have similar thoughts, hopefully you will get help for them before it turns into an "Almost" affair. I strongly believe that these sinful thoughts appear in the mind in small increments before they ever manifests in an actual affair. These steps are painful for me to divulge to you, but hopefully it is not in vain. Anyway, I knew what God and the Bible had to say about masturbation. I just didn't think I had any alternative at that point. In my mind, it was either masturbate or I would have an affair. I figured this was the lesser of the two evils. It's terrible to rationalize away my sinful acts.

About two months after my wife was diagnosed with cancer, I found myself talking to and flirting with more women. I would flirt with women at my old church. I would go over to their houses, secretly wishing they would comfort me. At first I just wanted to have someone else that was a woman that I could talk to and grieve with. You see, if I talked with my wife about her illness, she would get really upset and weep. I didn't want my wife to think about it or weep about it. So again in my mind, it was better to speak with others than to bring up this hard subject with my wife. When we are running from the hard stuff in life, it sure is hard to stay on track with our Christian walk! I would flirt with women at work. One of those women was the supervisor I told that I wanted to go home, and kill myself. My intent wasn't to harm myself, but to make her empathize with me. In turn, I was hoping it would bring us closer. I had surrounded myself with a lot of female friends. What I was really doing was trying to pick out a suitable replacement for my wife when she died. I was somehow hoping that the moment my wife passed away, one of these women could just move on into my house, and take over where she left off. Most of them were good listeners, but that's as far as it would ever go. In the back of my mind I wanted to have the physical act of sex with these women. I really didn't care about them or love them at all. I just wanted to physically satisfy my pain in my life. It was like Satan was on one shoulder, and God was on the other. They would keep whispering in my ear. Satan would say, "Your wife can't fulfill your needs, it's alright to find someone else to fulfill them. It doesn't mean you don't love your wife, but you can't adequately take care of your wife if you're sick as well." Then God would whisper in my ear, "Sex isn't everything in a marriage. Love your wife unconditionally, and be devoted wholly to just her." Man, I wanted to punch the devil off of one of my shoulders. I was just too weak to not listen. Quickly, dear reader, if you're not married this is one reason you want to wait until you're married to be sexually active. You don't really know if the guy loves you, or is just trying to fill a physical void in his life. You want to desperately believe he loves you, and I'm here to tell you in most cases it's not love at all! I have found this to be true. Women are more drawn to conversation than men are. Men really don't need much conversation to exist. Women on the other hand thrive on it for their existence. So when a man talks with, and listens to another woman, it stimulates them. It's a love language for a woman to be able to converse with a man. Well, this is another reason it's so dangerous to confide in a woman when things are not going well. But remember, guys don't really want to talk about touchy feely things, so when I did bring up stuff with other men they didn't want to engage. Since most men don't want to talk, and women do I, turned to them for my support. I also needed a hug to feel reassured in my grief. Guys are not into the whole hugging thing. The way men and women were made I think actually plays into how easy it is to be involved in an affair.

Soon taking care of my own urges was just not enough. My mind needed more in order to excite me. So I started to watch porn on my computer. It's so very hard to break these addictions. Oh how I wish it wasn't so easy to access this garbage. Oh how I wish that women didn't devalue themselves to the point to making these disgusting movies. I'm sure if I had a chance to speak with them and they were being honest, they would tell me it all started out with hurt in their lives. They took one baby step at a time until it got out of control as well. There's so much hurt in this world and so many things that Satan has in his arsenal to fill up this hurt. 1 Corinthians 10:13 says this: "No temptation has seized you except what is common to man. And God is faithful; he will not let you be tempted beyond what you can bear. But when you are tempted, he will also provide a way out so that you can stand up under it." This is a tough verse, because I was being tempted big time. It felt at the time that the temptations were too heavy for me to handle. It felt like I was hanging from a cliff, and God had his hand of the back of the collar of my shirt barely holding on. I know Satan was trying to push me off the cliff, and God still loved me, and had a plan for my life, so he was holding my feet to the cliff. I was bent on totally destroying myself and my marriage at the same time. God still loved me, and provided ways out. Was I walking in his perfect will? No! Was I living in a sinful lifestyle? Oh YES! However, anyone of these women could have gone through the actual physical act with me, but God was able to get me out before I committed the act itself. You will see soon, just how close I came from falling completely off the cliff.

The first year after my wife was diagnosed with terminal cancer was by far the worst in terms of spiritual warfare in my life. My attitude towards life was at an all time low. I was on anti-depressant medications to try to cope with life. When I wasn't working, I was sleeping the day away. To me, time would go by much faster while I was asleep. While asleep I didn't need to deal with the realities that were going on around me. I should have been more attentive to my wife's needs, but I couldn't muster the strength to care! It took all of my might to trudge through life. My views on life were marred by my wife's illness. My wife didn't do anything to deserve this, and neither did I. I felt like my wife getting sick was a punishment on me as well. The strong urge to feel loved by anyone seemed to permeate my whole being. When we're born we so desperately want to be held by our parents. When they held us as a baby we would stop crying, and smile back at them. I don't believe our internal need for being held and loved ever goes away, no matter how old we get. It is a big driving force in our lives. That driving force can be dangerous when we turn our face from God, and seek our own desires.

Let's get back to Bertha again. A little more than a year after my wife started going through chemo and radiation I received a phone call from Bertha. She was living in North Carolina at that time. She stated that she would be out to visit her parents in San Diego in a few weeks, and would like to see me. I could hardly wait to see Bertha again. I knew she was married with kids, so at that time I was not thinking anything would happen with her. I was just thinking that I was depressed and needed to open up to someone about my feelings. I needed someone I could trust to tell all of my hurts to that wouldn't chastise me for feeling the way I did. I had always felt through the years that I could tell Bertha anything, and she could do the same with me. The next two weeks seemed to go by so slowly while I was waiting for her to arrive. What she forgot to tell me was that her husband and kids were coming out to visit as well. I thought that this wouldn't permit me to have any time alone to speak to her. Little did I know at that time, that Bertha really wanted alone time to talk with me as well. That's a mixture for disaster!

Finally the day had arrived that I would get to see Bertha again. I arrived at Bertha's parents' home around 6 p.m. to eat dinner with their family. After dinner we sat around the house, and talked for about an hour. I enjoyed catching up with her family. Seeing her girls was a delight, since I hadn't met any of them up until then. Her girls were all cute, and looked just like their mother. The whole time I was still wondering if there was going to be any time where Bertha and I could be alone to talk. After an hour went by, Bertha actually asked me if I would like to go out for some dessert, and catch up on old times. Of course I didn't turn that down. We went to get some ice cream at a Dairy Queen. After that, I suggested that we go somewhere with a great view, where we could talk. I asked Bertha if she had to be back to her house at a certain time. I wanted to appear like I was being sensitive to her family's needs, but in actuality I didn't really care! Time was sure flying by that night. We were discussing what had happened in each other's lives in the past ten years since seeing each other. The subject matter that kept coming up that night was how neither of us was really happy with the lives we currently had. Both of us in different ways had been dealt a bad hand of cards, so we each felt. She was not happily married, and had wished things would have been different. I wanted so desperately to be happily married, but didn't know how that could ever happen with my wife being so ill. Dear reader, if you find yourself in a conversation where either you or the opposite sex person you're speaking with is unhappy with their life, leave immediately!

We arrived in my car to the overlook spot which was a well known romantic place. Fogged up car windows were the norm, not the exception at this place. We each got out of the car to marvel at the view. Then I remembered that I had a blanket in the trunk of my car. I retrieved it, and spread it out on the ground. We both sat down next to each other on the blanket. As we talked we would look into each other's eyes. My mind flashed back to when I was 16 years old again. Oh the love I felt for her at that time. Then Bertha said that it would have been better if she had married me instead of her husband. Red lights and sirens should have definitely gone off at this point. However, what she was saying was no longer being processed by my mind. We spoke to each other about our areas of hurt and pain. We both expressed the need to feel loved. Both of us felt that our relationships with our spouses were stagnant. God wasn't the center of either of our marriages at that time. My heart started to beat faster and faster. I was becoming so very nervous. I remember trembling and sweating as the conversation started to turn into "I miss, and love you!"

Remember the "Almost" kiss with Bertha? Well here's where it came back to haunt me. I had always thought about what it would have been like to kiss her that night ten years ago.. Now I was so nervous, but I brought that moment up to Bertha again. I said, "Bertha, the night in my car when I took you home, were you going to allow me to kiss you good night?" She said "yes" and that she was very disappointed that I didn't kiss her. She went on to say that it was one of the reasons she decided I was too young and immature for her. My heart was pounding even more, and my mind was only there for needed functions like breathing. I said, "Bertha I have thought about that night ever since, and what it would have been like to kiss you." Bertha then totally caught me off guard. She said, "You can kiss me now." Again, I knew the territory I was entering was not where God wanted me to be. My hurt was driving me forward. It was a good feeling and a terrible feeling all at the same time. I felt like I was betraying my wife, and God was watching the entire event unfold. That was a horrible feeling to have. However, my need to feel loved seemed to win out over who I was hurting. By the way I was also hurting myself, but definitely couldn't see that one at this time.

Before you knew it I was in full lip lock with Bertha. This was one of the most passionate kisses I have had in a long time. After this, Bertha said, "You know, you're a terrific kisser." Well, that was just what I needed to hear to boost my ego. Telling a hurting person that they are good at loving someone is not going to allow them to stop what they are doing. I asked if I could kiss her again. We had a long embrace, and continued kissing for the next hour or so. My brain was not even working at 1% at this time. Every rational thought shut done. I was only concerned at that point how to satisfy more of my sinful desires. The part of my body that had taken over my brain was only trying to find out how far we could take this new found infatuation.

After we had been there for about an hour and a half, I suggested that we head to a secluded portion of a beach, not too far away. She was all for a change of romantic venue. We held hands as we walked back to my vehicle and drove to the next beach. As soon as we arrived, we both got out to walk closer to the shore. There was not a soul in sight. By this time, we were losing track of time, but it was about 11p.m. The moon was full that night. It was beautiful as it danced on the waves rolling onto the shore. We sat down again and continued where we had left off. I began to feel there was no turning back. It was full steam ahead. For a brief moment, I thought about my wife Laura. My mind said I could deal with that problem later, and that what she didn't know wouldn't hurt her. I wasn't ever planning on telling her about this night. Thankfully, however, before things went any further, Bertha said she couldn't go any further than this. She slammed on the brakes hard. She obviously still had more of her brain working than I did. I had just come way to close to "Almost" having an affair. In God's eyes, and in my wife's eyes, this was an affair. I came to realize it was an affair even without the physical act being followed through much later on.

Well all the way home that night I was toiling in my mind over what I had done, and what I "Almost" did. It wasn't me that stopped me from going through the affair. If it would have been left up to me I would have had a physical affair. I was mad at myself for letting it get that far. The guilt was eating me up inside. How could I have done such a thing to my wife? If I didn't know God it would have probably been easy to just not say anything about it. You see, when you accept Christ into your life, you carry him everywhere you go. He can't be lied to or deceived. Even though I wasn't acting in a way that would be associated with being a Christ follower, I was being convicted in my soul by Christ. So when I got home I broke into tears. I told my wife I had to confess a terrible sin against her. I explained how I was being eaten up inside, and wanted to make this hurt go away. I thought the hurt that I had before this moment could be satisfied by filling it with another women's love. In the end it produced a much greater hurt. My wife was now hurt as well. Oh how I wish I could now take back that moment in time. The last person I wanted to hurt was my wife Laura. Laura rightfully was very upset. We did not speak to each other for at least a week. I slept on the couch, and she in the bedroom. I actually felt pretty fortunate that I wasn't booted from the house all together. You will see in the next chapter that this incident was not easy to just get over, even after apologizing. Today I'm thankful that God has given my wife the strength to completely forgive me as Christ did that very night.

To help summarize this chapter I want to look at James 1:13-15. It says, "When tempted, no one should say, God is tempting me. For God cannot be tempted by evil, nor does he tempt anyone, but each one is tempted when, by his own evil desire, he is dragged away and enticed." Then, after desire has conceived, it gives birth to sin, when it's full-grown, gives birth to death." You see, God isn't putting you into the places in life where you are tempted to sin. God didn't want me with Bertha that night at all. It was all my own desires and sin that got me to that place. I do believe because God didn't want me there he made a way for me to escape the full magnitude of the sinful situation. I was dragged away and enticed due to my selfish desires to fill an emotional void. Once this desire was conceived, it was hard to turn back. It in turn started out slowly then grew, and grew. When sin is allowed to be full grown, it leads to death. I believe that death is not only a separation from God's love in our life, but a separation from all of the people who love us. God didn't give us His commandments because he hates us. He gave us rules because he knows how much pain his children will be in if they don't listen to those rules. An earthly father tells his child not to run into the street, because the consequences could lead to death. God doesn't want you or me to enter the street named "affair". Because when you enter this street, if you don't make a quick u-turn back to God, it will lead to death. Thank you Jesus for allowing me to make a u-turn in my life!

Chapter 6 "Almost" got a divorce

When the word "divorce" comes from the lips of either spouse it cuts like a knife through the other's soul. Usually this word is thrown out when a lot of sinful activity is taking place in one or both of the individuals. When two people are living a life wholly devoted to Christ, the word "divorce" shouldn't come up. Sadly, some of the statistics that I have read lately show that divorce among Christians is the same as those outside the church. When you and I read this we should be asking ourselves what is going on to make this happen. I will be injecting some opinions as to why I believe divorce is rising in our society. You may not agree with me on all of them, so I apologize in advance if I offend you. My intent is not to make you angry with me, but for it to be thought provoking. Maybe you will have good discussions in your own church groups, because of some of the opinions I lay out. I will then go over several times in my own marriage where I would have to call it an "Almost" got divorced moment.

Well before we get to very far into this chapter I believe it's always important to again first see what God says about divorce. Matthew 5: 31-32 says, "It has been said, anyone who divorces his wife must give her a certificate of divorce. 'But I tell you that anyone who divorces his wife, except for marital unfaithfulness, causes her to commit adultery, and anyone who marries a woman so divorced commits adultery. So if neither of us is unfaithful then this verse states I can't get divorced. In Matthew 19: 3-9, God has a lot to say about divorce. It says, "Some Pharisees came to him to test him. They asked, 'Is it lawful for a man to divorce his wife for any and every reason?' 'Haven't you read', he replied, "that at the beginning the Creator made them male and female, and said, For this reason a man will leave his father and mother and be united to his wife, and the two will become one flesh? So they are no longer two, but one. Therefore what God has joined together, let man not separate.' 'Why then,' they asked, 'did Moses command that a man give his wife a certificate of divorce and send her away?' Jesus replied, 'Moses permitted you to divorce your wives because your hearts were hard. But it was not this way from the beginning. I tell you that anyone who divorces his wife, except for marital unfaithfulness, and marries another woman commits adultery.'" 1 Corinthians 7: 10-11 states, "To the married I give this command (not I, but the Lord): A wife must not separate from her husband. But if she does, she must remain unmarried or else be reconciled to her husband. And a husband must not divorce his wife." Malachi 2:16(a) says, "I hate divorce says the Lord God of Israel."

Well when the Lord says something once you say it might be a suggestion. When He says something twice, you start to think it could be important. But when He states something more than three times, He is hitting you and me over the head saying, "Hello, this is something important for you to understand!" Unless there is adultery involved, the word "divorce" shouldn't come up. I also want to stipulate that even if there is adultery involved, God still wants us to do whatever we can to be reconciled. Here is my opinion: if God didn't want us to reconcile, He most likely wouldn't tell us that we can't remarry again if we decide to divorce. After all, God made man first and then said it's not right for man to be alone. He made woman to be the man's helpmate. If two people divorce and must stay that way, there are going to be two very lonely people that God intended to be each other's mate forever. Malachi it sums it up well with God saying "I hate divorce". Now if God hates divorce, then why is it happening so much within our churches? In no way am I saying that divorce is a sin that is any worse than any other sin. I realize God died for the sin of divorce as well. However, Christians should be striving to be more Christ-like, not more like the world. Marriage must be an institution that must be taken more seriously by those who love the Lord.

Here are just a few reasons why I think divorce is on the rise. Just remember back to your grandparent's era. What were the statistics on divorce back then? Was it that your grandparents loved each other more, or was divorce just frowned on more? I believe the answer is yes to both. I'm not saying there weren't disagreements in marriages back then, but there was someone in the household that made the final decision. It was also harder to obtain a divorce in the past. Back when your grandparents were young, I imagine that the man worked and the woman stayed home. Again, I am making generalizations. By the way, I believe that a woman who stays home works just as hard as the man that goes outside the house to work. And whether you want to admit it or not, God intended man to do the more laborious stuff. God intended a different role for men then he did for women. There is just one small tiny difference in the relationship. God called man to be the head of the household. What that means is that the woman is "Almost" equal to the man. In my marriage, I try whenever possible to go out of my way to please my wife. When a very tough decision has to be made, I try to see it her way if at all possible. There have been rare occasions that I have had to make a decision that is contradictory to my wife's. However a marriage can't work if one person doesn't have the ability to have the final say. Both people can't be chief - it just plain don't work. Just think about your work situation. Aren't there supervisors over you, and over them are higher supervisors? Each of them has a role, and a greater responsibility. God calls the man to a higher responsibility in the role of marriage. I believe that a significant change occurred in our society when both husband and wife began working outside the home. Now there are two people in the same house earning money. Both want to have equal say, since there is equal work being done. In general I believe the church has gotten away from teaching what the man's role is versus what the women's role is in the household. This line has become so blurred. It is now taboo to say that a woman must "submit" to a man. Why? It shouldn't be considered a dirty word, if God says a man should love his wife just as Christ has loved the Church. We have different roles. When we don't accept those roles that God intended, then the consequence manifests itself in higher divorce rates!

Our churches today are bending the rules when it comes to divorce. In 1 Timothy 3: 12 it says, "A deacon must be the husband of but one wife and must manage his children and his household well. It's pretty clear to me that our leaders within the church are called to a higher standard. I'm not saying that all churches waiver on this, but if I'm seeing it happen in churches today, it has to be more prevalent. If the church doesn't have consequences for divorce then what's to stop people from divorcing? If the church just slaps someone on the wrist and tells them to carry on with what they are doing because all is forgiven, then the divorce rate is going to continue to rise within the church. Here is another opinion – being forgiven does not mean there will be no consequences. If a person kills another person, the consequence is either the death sentence, or life in prison. If that same man truly finds God and accepts him into his heart while in prison does this man go to heaven? Most certainly he is forgiven for the sin, but do we let him out of prison? No, that's the consequence for sin. All throughout the Bible we see consequence for sin. David's baby was taken by God due to his sin. God restored David after that. So if a person is truly repentant for their sin, of course we forgive them. We love them. However we can only try to restore them to a certain point, where God draws the line. So many people in church don't believe there is a line. I run into people all the time that say God is love. They often forget he is also a jealous, wrathful God. He is a God that can't look on sin. If a leader in the church divorces, do we kick them out? No way! They need to be loved like Christ still loves them. This believer just needs to be counseled appropriately as to why the consequences are what they are. I'm sure by now I have ruffled some of my reader's feathers. I'm quite sure that many of my ideas, and opinions won't be preached in church. But I'm saying these things anyway, because I love the church. I want to see the church as a shining light for the world. In order for that to happen, hard things need to be said and dealt with. I hope at the very least you will ponder and discuss these things amongst fellow believers.

Dear reader, are you still with me? Whew!! I thought I might lose you after the first few pages of this chapter. Thanks for hanging in there with me! I'm now going to get into the meat of my "Almost" divorce moments. Growing up in a Christian home, I rarely saw my parents argue. When they had a disagreement, their voice didn't elevate. It's calming to live in a household where two parents love each other very much. I was fortunate enough to see how marriage was supposed to be firsthand. I remember my dad giving me some great advice about having a healthy, happy, long lasting marriage. He said, "Don't ever let the word "divorce" come from your mouth." He also gave me this verse: Ephesians 4:26-27, which says, "In your anger do not sin: Do not let the sun go down while you are still angry, and do not give the devil a foothold." This was some really great advice from my dad who, continues to live out what a true Christian marriage should be. My dad told me that if the word "divorce" comes out in conversation, even if it's in a joking manner, it will eventually become anything but a joke. It's like the boy who cried wolf. After awhile, each person gets used to hearing that word, and subconsciously begins to accept the idea of it. You see at first you use the word divorce to manipulate your partner by fear to change whatever it is you think is wrong with them. It might work for the short term. However, once you utter this terrible nasty word too many times, the fear wears off. Your partner gets tired of being bullied into things by fear and they start to call your bluff. They will say, "Great, I'm tired. Let's just get divorced. Once your partner calls your bluff, you have only two options. Get a divorce, because your trump card no longer works. Or get counseling to fix the issues in the marriage, and move forward together. The latter of those two takes much more work. I just used the bad word – "work". If you want to have a long marriage, it will take a lot of work! There is no real way around it! If hard work

147

scares you, then my advice is don't get married!

I'd like to look at Ephesians 4:26-27 again, as it offers us so much wisdom. First, it says, "In your anger do not sin." It doesn't say "if" or "when" you get angry. It says "in" your anger. God already knows that two people that are struggling to be one flesh aren't always going to see things eye to eye. It's what you do and how you react in the times of disagreement that determine the course of your marriage. The verse goes on to say, "don't let the sun go down while you're still angry." I believe this literally means not go to sleep that night without resolving whatever disagreement the two of you may have had. What does it look like when you fall asleep angry? Well, I will tell you what happens in my house. If we've gone to sleep without settling a disagreement, I'm lucky if I'm even sleeping in our bed that night.. If I am, then I would be on the edge of the opposite side from my wife. and my body would be facing away from her. This is what is meant in the next verse where it says don't give the devil a foot hold. When both people are facing in the opposite direction they can't be one flesh. When they are not one flesh, there is a lot of space between them where Satan can come in and place a wedge. I look at a wedge as a huge splinter in the relationship. When a splinter is in your hand, and you don't take it out, what happens? The area starts to fester, and get infected. Once it's infected, puss starts to come out. If you don't take care of this infection, it will either take your hand, or your life. The same thing happens in marriage. Leave that giant wedge in between two people for too long, and infection of the heart sets in. The puss part is when the two people start to spew hurtful words at each other. If still left untreated by Godly professional counseling, then death arrives in the form of divorce!

In my life I sure wish I could tell you that I have always followed the rules, and heeded the advice I received from my father. Believe me, it's always easier said than done because it is something you actually have to work at. When I got married I was sure in my mind that I would never throw out the word "divorce". I told myself that no matter how hard things got, I won't go that far. Well, I believe I got to about the 1 ½ year mark of my marriage before that word left my lips. I was ashamed that I allowed myself to hurt my wife in this way. My wife has always had a problem with her weight. The problem just kept getting worse, so we would at first have discussions about how it hurt me that she was overweight. My wife didn't ever consider her weight to be a problem for her, so it was only my problem. Soon those discussions got to be more hurtful. I would say things like, "You don't turn me on anymore", or, "I'm young, and deserve a woman that cares about the up keep of her body", or, "Other people make fun of me, and say hurtful things like 'Can't you do better than her?'" My wife was getting really fed up with me nagging her about her weight. One day when I brought up the subject again she said, "If you don't like it you can leave." She didn't say the bad word, but she was alluding to it. So I said, "Alright, if you want a divorce I will give you one." This was the first time that an "Almost" divorce took place. This was a result of me harping on her weight. Some things are just not that important to argue about in the first place. Since this was really the first time divorce came up, it wasn't taken seriously, and we continued on with our marriage. From this point on, I very rarely brought up the weight issue, even though it still affected me deeply. I just knew at that time it was a sore subject, and I stayed away from it. But just simply avoiding a painful subject isn't the best course of action. It still eats away and festers inside that person. Eventually, it will come back up and may be even worse than the first time. Don't wait for counseling. Get help while the problem is still a relatively small one in each other's heart.

After being married about 3 years, I found myself out of work. My wife was still working, and was now the chief bread winner in the household. This situation caused me many sleepless nights. Up until then both of were working full time, and still barely making ends meet. We were still in debt from the poor choices we made in the past, like gambling. Even with two incomes, we were barely able to pay the minimum balances on everything we owed. We were now both in way over our head. The strife and tension that's created by a lack of money is horrible. I believe the two main causes of failed marriages are financial hardship, and infidelity. I believe God speaks about money more than anything else in the Bible, so He knows it's a major issue with us. Laura and I have had terrible arguments about money, sometimes lasting into the next day. For example, Laura was upset with me for not being able to find another job. Eventually this led us to have to file for Chapter 7 bankruptcy. We just couldn't keep up with our finances. Losing your credit and ability to have expendable cash wreaks havoc on relationships. Before filing for bankruptcy, I thought it would be better if I just divorced my wife. Most of the credit cards were in my name, not my wife's name. I was actually given advice from several people that it would be wise of me to divorce my wife, and then claim bankruptcy to mitigate the financial damages on both people. Horrible advice givers are out there all over the place. When you are in trouble seek Godly professionals to get advice from. My wife didn't know until much later how close I was to filing for divorce, due to the financial situation we were in. This was another "Almost" got divorced moment.

When Laura was diagnosed with terminal brain cancer in January of 2001, the thoughts of divorce went through my head constantly. When a spouse gets a terminal illness at a young age, statistics say the marriage is doomed. The sick spouse is now going to suck the life out of the other person. The spouse that's not ill needs to be more selfless, and must take over the other person's previous responsibilities.. In your mind you don't see the scenario playing out well. I didn't want to be a caretaker for my dying wife at a young age. I thought about just letting one of her family members watch over her until she passed away. Part of that was selfishness, and the other was that I simply didn't believe I could handle the hardship of it all. The longer my wife would live, the more of me that would die each day. I felt I was still young enough to attract a normal healthy woman. I wanted so desperately to have a normal life with a normal wife. In a nut shell, my soul was in torment over my wife being terminally sick. I was doing some investigation into divorce attorneys, so I was definitely giving it some serious thought. I had a good Godly friend give me some good advice. They asked me if I meant it when I vowed before God to take care of my wife in sickness and in health. I said, "Yah, but…" I was cut off immediately without the ability to get my "but" out. The question was repeated. I said, "Well yes." Then they asked if I meant it when I said "until death do I part." I tried the "but" thing again, and was cut off. "Did you mean it, yes, or no?" I said, "Yes, I meant it." "Well, you need to be the man God wants you to be. Most men would give up in your situation, but most men don't do the Godly thing. How will you be defined by God's standards, or the world's standards?" What this friend had said really struck me hard. If you know me, you will know that I specifically chose my wedding band because it has a cross of diamonds on a gold band. I chose this because when I looked down at my finger, I wanted it to remind me that I wasn't just saying my vows to my wife, but to God. If I meant them, then I must mean them now when the rubber meets the road. We can't live in a "what if" mode, but rather a "God mode", when the trials of life take place. This was another time where I "Almost" divorced my wife.

The night that I confessed to Laura about my romantic interlude with Bertha was a tough night. The word "divorce" came up with vigor on this night, and for many nights to follow. I couldn't blame my wife for wanting a divorce in this instance. Even though the physical act of an affair didn't take place, in God's eye's it was still an affair. In my mind I already had the affair, and in my heart as well. Such a betrayal in a marriage is very hard to overcome. How did we make it through this "Almost" divorceable moment? Well it took a tremendous amount of work, and groveling on my part to convince Laura to stay with me. Marriage was already hard work before I messed up. Now it was extremely hard work. Not only was I trying to repair a broken heart, I was also trying to restore the trust between two married people. Now when I got to work every day, I would call Laura to tell her when I arrived. I didn't really go anywhere except for work without Laura. My phone calls were at a minimum, and my wife now had access to the people I called. I had to put these things into place to build that trust back into our relationship. God told me not to travel down this road. I did it anyway, and I reaped the consequences of getting run over. After about 6 months my wife finally said she had forgiven me, and it was time to move on. We vowed to not bring it up again, but unfortunately that's easier said than done. Now I'm bringing it up again as well, but this time in hopes that it keeps someone else from the heartache it caused me. That first month afterwards was filled with a lot of we "Almost" got divorced moments.

A couple of years went by before we hit the biggest hurdle in our marriage. You would have thought that "Almost" having an affair would have been the straw that broke the camel's back right? I think this incident was just the icing on the cake. Even though someone says that they forgive you, the painful event is always in the back of their mind. Only God can truly forgive our sins as far as the east is from the west. When water starts to boil, it bubbles harder and harder until either it boils over, or someone turns the heat down. I thought that we adequately turned the heat down with what had happened, but it turned out that it wasn't dealt with properly. One rainy day my wife called me, and told me that she had just been in an accident. She said she ran into the rear of another car. The first question out of my mouth was "How is my car?" I should have asked if she was injured. I should have asked how she was doing, and what I could do to help her out. But what she heard was that I was more concerned with how the car was than how she was. What was going through my head, was she is obviously fine, because if she wasn't, she wouldn't have called me in the first place. I felt that I could skip the "how are you", and get to the car at that time. My way of thinking was insensitive to my wife. She immediately felt that I loved the car more than I loved her. In her mind at that point, it was the last straw.

Now Laura was actively seeking the divorce. She called her dad to explain everything to him. He said if she wanted a divorce, he would get her a good attorney, and pay for it. I was very scared now. Laura was serious enough to involve her dad. She never told her dad about our disagreements before. It had always just been up to us to work out our problems. Now she was seeking advice on how to end the marriage. Not only that, her dad was willing to pay for the whole process, and make sure she got a good attorney. I was thinking, "Man, this is going to cost me big time!" I knew having two children that child support would cost a small fortune. I thought my wife was blowing the whole situation out of proportion. Just because I didn't ask her how she was doing before asking about the car in my mind didn't mean I didn't love, or care for her. I begged her again to reconsider. Our pastor gave us the name of a Christian counselor. We each went to this counselor about four times. We started to discuss things in our sessions that we each had said we forgave the other for in the past. It turned out that the past wasn't really in the past yet. Everything came out into the open, from her illness, to her weight and my "Almost" affair. The counselor actually told my wife she had good grounds for a divorce. Still today I'm not quite sure how a Christian counselor could say such a thing? She at least caused us to openly discuss everything we were upset about. We both cried a lot as we opened up to each other. Pain is sometimes a necessity to get to a resolution in ones lives. The counselor's fee was $90.00 an hour, so we made sure we got better in a hurry! This was the closest we ever came to "Almost" getting a divorce, and thankfully it was also the last time.

I would like to offer some opinions on how to avoid "Almost" getting divorced in. I offered a few already, like not letting the sun go down on your anger, so as not to let the devil get a foothold. Here are some other practical ways to keep your marriage on the right track. First, make your wedding anniversary a big deal. Marriage is hard work, and you need to take time to thank your spouse for all of the hard work they put into the marriage over the past year. Don't think of it as just another year gone by. God values marriage, and so should we. God rejoices when we stay married, so we need to celebrate that as well. Second, surprise your spouse with an "I love you gift" throughout the year. It doesn't have to be flowers. Anything that says "I love you" will do. Do this at times of the year other than Valentine's Day, or your spouse's birthday. Do this when you're not just making up for a moment you blew it. Do this just because you love your spouse. Often when kids come along in a relationship we forget to take time out for ourselves. The kids came after the marriage, so make sure you never lose sight that your love for each other came first.. You were with each other before kids, and Lord willing will be together long after the kids leave home. You will need to find a good babysitter, or family member you can trust to watch your kids. You then need to make a scheduled date night. We tend to schedule everything else in our lives, but neglect to schedule in our spouses for attention. Try to get away to do something one time a month. It can be as simple as dinner for just the two of you. Once a year, try to take a small vacation away from the kids, even if it's for a whole day. I know this next suggestion will sound weird, but it works. The two of you need to make sure you schedule time for romantic interludes. Now, if it happens spontaneously at other than scheduled times, then that's a great bonus. However, I find that people get so busy that they aren't that spontaneous anymore. Trust me, if you schedule romantic times together and stick to them, your relationship will stay on good ground. Peers can also have a huge role in the health of your marriage. Surround yourselves with other couples that have healthy marriages. Find couples that have been married for a lot longer than you have. They will have already been through the pot holes of life, and can give you the proper advice on how to avoid them. Cheer on those that are married. When they have an anniversary, be excited for them. Give them praise. Society doesn't give enough praise to those that are doing it right.

I want to thank my parents Mil & April for being such a good example of a Godly married couple. They have been married for 43 years! Both sets of my grandparents also remained married to the same spouse. I have been privileged to be a part of such a good legacy. There is also a very Godly couple that everyone looks up too at my church in Mesa, Arizona. The couple I'm speaking of is Wally & Doris Robbins, and they have been married for 63 years! They both have a smile from ear to ear whenever I see them. They hold hands in public. There's no doubt that they genuinely still love each other as much today as they did the day they said "I do". They tell me that in all the time they have been married, they have never had a serious argument.. I'm sure if you look hard enough, you too can find the Wally & Doris in your own life. Get to know them, and let them help you out on your journey in marriage. Believe me, people like this don't stay married by chance. They know the recipe for success in marriage, and they would love to share it with you!

Chapter 7 "Almost" won an election.

About three years ago is when I decided to run for a political office. At the time I was working for an insurance company. Part of my duties for this insurance company was to file court documents.. One day while I was at court, I ran into a guy that was wearing cowboy boots, jeans, a western shirt and a cowboy hat. That in itself isn't what intrigued me the most. It was that he was also wearing a gun belt, and a badge. I thought, "What type of law enforcement officer is this laid back?" I went up to introduce myself to him. He told me that he was a constable for the justice courts. He stated he loved his job, because it gave him great flexibility during the day. He explained to me briefly what his duties were. I said to myself, "This is a job I know I am qualified to do, and would also enjoy it!" When I went home later that day I started to look up more information about constables, and their duties.

I was a little disappointed with my original research. In order to be a constable, one must live in the city that they wish to run for. The term for a constable is four years long. However, not every city has their constable come up for re-election at the same time. I decided that I wanted to run for constable in the city of Chandler, AZ. A year prior was when the last election was held. What this meant for me was I had to wait for "Almost" three years to run for this political position. If you remember back to Chapter 2 where I talk about "Almost" getting my dream job, you will understand that this would be an opportunity to obtain that dream. This would be a law enforcement position that fit me perfectly. It had been so long since I had tried to get into law enforcement. Now I would have to wait another two years before I could even throw my hat into the ring, and a year after that for the vote. Waiting has never been one of my strengths.

You're probably asking what does a constable even do. Constables are an integral part of the justice court system in Arizona. The constable is an elected official who serves as the executive branch of the courts. Constables serve all processes given to them by the justice of the peace. The process includes service of criminal and civil subpoenas and summonses, writs of restitution (eviction orders), writs of execution (orders to collect judgments), writs of replevin (orders to seize property), orders of protection and injunctions against harassment as well as any other orders from the courts. Constables may also be involved in the sale of seized property and summoning jurors for trials. I had already gained a lot of experience in the area of process serving subpoenas, and the rest I was confident I could learn to do quickly.

For the next two years I was in a holding pattern. That didn't mean that I didn't do anything to try to prepare for running. I went down to the Maricopa County Recorder's office to get information on how to run for office. There is a big packet of information that a person needs to be familiar with before actually running for office. Was I going to have a treasurer, and raise money for the campaign? If I decided to take donations, what were the rules on this? What were the tax implications? Did I need a campaign manager to help with all of the details? Believe when I say this the process can be a nightmare. Eventually

I decided to run my campaign without a treasurer. I would run my campaign under a $500 threshold rule. This rule meant that I could only accept up to $500 from other's for my campaign, and no more than that. I could spend as much of my own personal money on the campaign as I wanted though. Being that this was my first time running for a political office, the whole financial area of how to handle donations really scared me! This would be a true grass roots campaign. That meant that I would have to do everything myself, with no outside support. I found out much later that politicians don't run these types of campaigns much anymore.

While doing my research, I found out who the current constable of Chandler was. He had been a constable for about 10 years. His father was the constable for many years before him. There was a long legacy of constables in this person's family. Not only that, he was a Republican, and so am I. It would have been much easier to find an office that was vacant, or run against a democrat than to go up against such strong opposition. I knew it was going to be a huge uphill climb to take on someone so established. I did worry that I was biting off way more than I could chew. One thing about me though, is no matter how much the odds are stacked against me, when I put my mind towards something I don't back down. I will have to say that can be a strength, but it can in some cases be a great weakness. I was the little guy on the play ground deciding to pick a fight with the giant. It was a classic David vs. Goliath! The current constable was still young, so there wasn't a chance of him retiring. I really didn't know if the current constable was good at his job. I didn't know if he had done anything wrong while in his position. Quite frankly, I didn't care about my opponent's strengths or weaknesses. I only knew that if I focused on my strengths, it would be enough to win the election. I have always felt that if a person must put down someone else in order to win, then they themselves don't have any positive attributes. Wouldn't it be nice if all politicians were strong enough to run without throwing mud at the other person?

In November, two months before I could officially run for office, I came to the Lord on my knees, and said something like this: "Lord, you know that in my heart I would like to be in law enforcement. Lord up until this point you have closed this door in my life. Lord, if this is where you want me to be then let this process continue, but if this is not your will, don't let it come to pass." I was praying a James 1:5 prayer, where it says, "If any of you lacks wisdom, he should ask God, who gives generously to all without finding fault, and it will be given to him." I had tried so many times in the past to kick the door down myself in terms of getting my dream job. I didn't want to have that approach again, so I completely gave it to God. I had been hurt so many times in the past, and I just felt I couldn't go down that road again. I was seeking ultimate guidance from God in this process.

No doors had shut on me as of yet so, when January rolled around I went back to the Maricopa County Recorder's office. At that time, I picked up a large packet of information. I was extremely excited about starting the process. I spent the rest of that day reading through, and filling out all of the necessary paperwork to run for constable. The very next day I went back to the records office to turn in all of my paperwork. While I was there, all of my paperwork was checked over to make sure I had done everything correct. It was then notarized, and date stamped to make it official. Putting in this paperwork was the easy part. Anybody can turn in their application in to run, but it doesn't count if that candidate doesn't have the necessary amount of signatures backing them up. I was given a blank petition sheet for signatures. Each petition sheet held 15 signatures. Each line needed to have the printed name, signature, address and date of each registered voter. I didn't know how many signatures that I needed to collect. The information I originally found indicated about 600 signatures would be the minimum, so I would make sure I had around 750. I took the blank petition sheet to Kinko's to make copies. I had 50 copies run off, which would get me the amount I thought I needed. The recorder's office wouldn't officially post the exact amount needed until April 1st. I also sent a family photo to a printing company where I had 5,000 business cards printed up. My plan was to hand a business card out to everyone that I met. To this day, I believe I have 3,000 business cards still left over. So a little over kill on my part. I was now able to start this tedious process.

Now every signature is not a counting signature. Since I'm a registered Republican, I could only get signatures from people that are registered Republicans, Independents or Undecideds. I didn't think this would be that big of a deal. I just had to ask each person I came across what party they were affiliated with. Now I knew I needed a lot of signatures, and I didn't want this process to take a whole lot of time. Oh how naïve I was at how this process worked! When I was growing up, I remember seeing people standing outside the DMV and supermarkets to collect political signatures. So naturally, I thought it would be very easy to stand in front of a store or the DMV, and get my signatures. I was very wrong! As it turns out, people don't want anything to do with politicians any longer. They believe it's bad for business to have a politician standing outside. I would challenge store owners, by telling them that I've seen the girl scouts outside their business selling cookies, and I'm not selling anything, so why can't I be here? Now don't get me wrong, I like the girl scouts, and I buy cookies from them all the time. I was just trying to figure out why them, and not me. I was told several times that nonprofit organizations are ok, but they didn't want a politician within a mile of their establishment. I was finding out firsthand how people's view of politicians had really gone down the drain. I was being treated like the plague. My view of politicians was tainted, but not to this extreme, not yet anyway!

Well I had to find a better way to get my signatures. I was informed that the main library in Chandler might help me. I drove over to the library to get permission to get signatures in front of their establishment. You think it was that easy? Nope! I was given a map of where I could and couldn't stand. As it turned out, I was not allowed to be on library property. I had to stand on the other side of a concrete barrier, which was actually state park property. This meant I had to raise my voice to get the attention of the people passing by. It also meant that these people would really have to go out of their way to come over and sign my petition. There were also others at the same place vying for signatures like I was. Evidently, people used this spot for petition signatures for everything under the sun. I also found out that most people that you see going to the library are actually the same ones over, and over again. Most of these people were plain tired of being hounded for signatures, so most would ignore me. Immediately, I knew this was not going to be easy. I stood outside the library for 3 hours, and got a whopping 20 signatures. I stood in front of the library for the first week and a half. I would spend almost all day on Saturday at the library. I was only averaging 7 signatures an hour. Thinking that I needed 700 signatures, I that this was going to take 100 hours to get this completed. I had to search for a faster way to get the signatures. There had to be a way. Then one day, someone at the library told me how to get plugged into the Republican Party website. This website housed all of the registered voters by party affiliation.

I called the people that controlled the website and I was sent a packet of information to fill out, so that I could be granted access to this website. Once I filled out the paperwork, I faxed it all to the administrator. They did a quick background check to make sure I wasn't a criminal. The information I was being given access to was very sensitive. I also had to sign paperwork stating I would only use this website for political reasons, and not to try to sell anything to anyone. A week later, I was given a password, and granted access to this website. I was now able to check the signatures that I had already gotten at the library against this data base. I was very disappointed to find that only about 3 out of every 7 signatures were good. As it turns out, a lot of people either didn't know whether they were registered to vote, or they didn't really know what party they belonged too. Since I was only getting an average of 3 signatures per hour, it was going to be even harder to get the signatures that I needed.

Someone also suggested that I contact the person in charge of the Republican Party in Chandler. Once I found out whom this person was, I gave them a call and set up a lunch appointment with them Before retiring, this person had been a successful career politician. I was very excited to meet him. Surely, I thought, he would be able to give me the guidance needed to get my campaign going. When we finally met over lunch, he asked me if I had ever run for office before. My answer was "no". Then he wanted to know why I was running for constable. I told him why, and then he said, "You do realize that you're running against someone that has been in this position for a long time, and his father was constable before that." I said I did know this information. He then asked how much money I was willing to spend to run my campaign. I told him that I was currently unemployed and couldn't afford to spend more than $250.00 to run my campaign. The gentlemen began to laugh. He said that my opponent would spend tens of thousands of dollars to keep his seat. If I wasn't prepared to spend that kind of cash, I really had no chance of winning. He told me that he had been in politics for 40 years, and he has never seen anyone win a race without spending a lot of money. He sure busted my bubble. Here I thought that if I worked hard enough, money wouldn't be an issue. Sadly, the person that has the most money is rarely really looking out for the best interest of the voters. They didn't get rich by helping others, but by finding loop holes to help themselves get richer. Still this gentleman I was having lunch with invited me to go to the monthly Republican meeting. He said that I would be able to get up in front of the group, and speak for 5 minutes. He told me that there would be political committeemen that would be there, and their sole purpose was to help candidates get signatures.

When the night of the republican meeting finally arrived I was excited. I anticipated meeting a lot of new people that could help me in my endeavor to become a constable. When I arrived I was told that the 5 minutes I would get to speak was not going to be a reality. They would try to give me 30 seconds on the docket, but a more important candidate was coming to the meeting. This candidate was nationally known. A big deal was made about it with CNN covering this event. This politician sat next to me at this event. Interestingly, he had earlier professed to be a Christian. But while sitting next to this person and listening to him speak to his political advisor, I didn't see his walk matching his talk. I had met several prominent people that day. They all shook my hand and smiled. They all said, "Nice to see you again!" I had never met these people in my life. It was a bunch of people that were totally fake with each other. I was told later that this is called "glad handing" - it's similar to kissing babies. The more I spoke with the politicians, the angrier I got. It actually gave me a sick feeling in the pit of my stomach. I thought to myself, "Is this really how people see me as well?" I was seeing firsthand how the American public was being duped into believing the lies coming from these peoples lips. I'm making a very broad statement based on what I saw that night, I know. I'm sure that somewhere there is a good, upstanding, true Christian politician. While at this meeting I was instructed to pass my petition around the room for signatures. After about a hundred people touched it, I got it back with two signatures on it. At the end of the meeting I was told I could stand in the back of the room, and ask political committeemen to help me get signatures for my campaign. I was informed by several of them that the person I was running against was also Republican, and they were already backing him. This was a major setback for me. Every time I was told I would get some help, I found a road block. Of course, the political party wanted me to still go out and campaign for other candidates, but they were not going to back me. This quest to "Almost" win an election was starting to wear me down!

Before I started to run for this office, I was sure that I would get backing from the church. Fellow Christians were always complaining that the people in office lacked moral turpitude. All I needed to do was to meet with pastors of churches, and I was positive to get signatures that I needed. I knew that if the Christians could get to know me, I would garner their vote. I started making calls to churches. In most cases, I had to call back several times before getting a response. I finally got a couple of meetings with pastors of large churches. I asked them for permission to stand outside their sanctuary and speak with their members as they left. I asked if it would be alright to get signatures. I had already checked into the legality of what I was asking of them. I didn't want the church to lose their tax exempt status, so I couldn't ask the pastor to endorse me from the pulpit. As long as they didn't endorse me from the pulpit, it was legal for me to get signatures outside. Even armed with this knowledge, the pastors all told me they would have to check with their attorney. Each of them came back to me stating that although it wasn't illegal, they didn't want to align themselves with any political candidate. Then each of them prayed that God would help me out. I was crushed to my core. It felt like the church had already given up on backing Christians in politics. In my opinion, the reason we are seeing laws going on the books like legalizing gay marriage is because the church is taking a back seat! The church is sitting around waiting for the end times to come. Believe me dear reader, the end will come, but let God figure out the timing of the end. In the meantime, we still need to fight for biblical principles in our society. You will see in the next chapter that this became a moment where I "Almost" gave up on God.

Well I now knew I was going to have to do this journey alone. I "Almost" gave up at this point. Then when I was reading the scriptures, I came across this verse that I felt spoke directly to me at that time. Hebrews 12:1 says, "Therefore, since we are surrounded by such a great cloud of witnesses, let us throw off everything that hinders and the sin that so easily entangles, and let us run with perseverance the race marked out for us." Since there were witnesses in heaven pulling for me, I couldn't quit. Every road block I hit was something that tried to hinder me. The sin was all around me in different forms. It felt as if Satan didn't want a Christian to run in this race. I felt like Satan was trying to discourage me however he could to get me to quit. I "Almost" got entangled with it all. I felt that for some reason God wanted me to persevere. I had to trust God's bigger plan in this, and I continued to forge ahead in this race.

Needing a way to find qualified voters to sign my petition, I went back to the data base I now had access to. I was able to put in certain parameters, and print out a walking list in different parts of the city. Because these people were on the voter rolls, I already knew their signatures would be good. What I didn't know was the data base was very out dated. There were people on the list that died over five years ago. It's quite embarrassing to knock on someone's door, and ask the wife or husband if their dead relative would like to sign my petition! Even though the list was only about 80% correct, it was the best tool I had at my disposal. I would start at about 4 p.m. at night Monday-Saturday. I would drive to the different neighborhoods on my walking list and go door to door I was averaged 7 signatures per hour doing this. This was still not a very fast way to get signatures, but I knew at least they all counted. Each night I would walk 2.5 to 3.5 miles knocking on doors. By the time I got all of the needed signatures, I figured I had walked over 195 miles. I was also spending an extra $30 a week in gas, driving to all the neighborhoods. The more I looked at the cost and the odds, of being elected, the more I would tell my wife that I should give this ridiculous dream up. My wife would encourage me to keep going, and do what God wanted me to do.

If you have ever knocked on doors to ask for anything from people, you will know what type of internal fortitude that takes. If you're a shy person then stay away from knocking on doors. Most nights when I got done walking the neighborhood, my mental attitude was very low. This process was took a physical and mental toll on me. A lot of people in this world are so angry at everything. If a person comes to their door, they take out all of their anger out on that person. People would ask me how I dare interrupt them while they're busy. I would usually be quick to say, "I'm so sorry my ESP was turned off recently, so I didn't know that you were busy." I was cursed out more times than I could count. Doors were slammed in my face. The times it made me the saddest were when people had a scripture reading posted outside their door, and they didn't act at all like they knew Christ! People always assumed I was either selling them something, or I was a Jehovah's Witness. After about a month of walking door to door on my own my wife, and kids offered to go with me. My wife would drive me from street to street to make it easier on me. My kids would take turns walking door to door. It was funny, my kids could only do about half of the walking I did each night before they would complain about being too tired. It made me feel good that I was still in good shape at my age. But I also found out something very interesting when my kids joined me. I was very scared at first at letting my kids walk with me, because of the foul language I would receive. However, when my kids were with me, more people opened their doors to me. More people signed my petition. A whole lot less cursing and door slamming was going on. People acted more civilized when my children were around. I wondered if these people realized that God was always present, even when my kids weren't. Try to remember that wherever you go. God is there. That should have an effect on the way we act towards others. I was now getting about 10 signatures per hour, so things were looking up.

About three months into the process, I had 400 signatures and was feeling pretty good. I still thought at that time that if I got around 700 signatures, it would be enough. Well the day came where the Recorder's office website posted the exact number of signatures I would need. The number blew me away. I had to look at that number for a few seconds due to my disbelief. The magic number needed to get me on the ballot was 1,086 signatures. I had always been told that I should have at least 20% more than the required amount of signatures, because some of the signatures wouldn't be verifiable. I was also instructed that my opponent would challenge every single one of my signatures. When someone registers to vote they have to sign their name. If my opponent were to challenge my signatures, and the person didn't sign the exact way that they did when they registered, the signature wouldn't count. I was already not very trusting of the whole political process. I just knew it was all rigged somehow. Now I felt that I would need a minimum of 1,300 signatures to make sure all of my hard work was not in vain. I now had 4 months to get 900 signatures, and I had just got 400 in about 3 months. That meant I really had to step up my time commitment each day to get the needed signatures.

I started spending even more time walking the neighborhood. I went from walking 2.5 -3.5 miles a night, to walking at least 3.5-4.0 miles a night. I went from getting about 15 signatures a day to 22-25 signatures a day. Being in Arizona, it was starting to get very hot outside towards the end of my signature gathering. Every time I went out knocking on doors, I wore a dress shirt, tie and suit jacket. People would always ask me if I was hot, and why I was wearing a tie. My response was that first impressions are lasting impressions. I knew that most of these people they would never see me again. I had to put a positive image into their mind quickly. I wanted them to know that I was a professional, and was asking for their trust in me to do the job I was running for. Would anyone want to vote someone into office that didn't look nice?

Most people would say they were surprised that the actual person running would be out knocking on doors themselves. I think one of the reasons I came close to "Almost" winning an election, is because people met the real candidate and not a helper. My brother and sister-in-law were living in town for some of the time I was running for office. They were able to generously spend some hours on a few Saturday's to get about 150 signatures for me. I'm grateful for their help

What was my attitude through this process? I went through a lot of high and low periods mentally. On one hand, I felt that God wanted me to keep going. On the other hand, I wasn't getting much help from anyone. I didn't feel like anyone was willing to back me in this difficult quest. I felt pretty alone most of the time. It was me and my family doing this all by ourselves. Often times I did not feel like getting on my shirt and tie and going to knock on doors. I would say to my wife, "You know I'm just wasting my time. This whole thing is a big waste of time." In my low moments I wouldn't feel like I was worth very much. Here I was devoting all of this time for something that would probably not pan out. I felt that no matter what I tried in my life, I had failed at it. I so desperately wanted to finally succeed at something. I would also tell my friends what I was doing. I would tell them how hard it was to get the required signatures. I was told several times that they would pray for me. Now remember, when I was mentally and physically beat up, my mind didn't think clearly. I was frustrated with all of my friends who were willing to pray for me, but who were not willing to give up any of their time to help me out. All they are willing to do is pray! Again, I believe in the power of prayer, but without works, it's dead! What I heard my friends telling me was, "We hope you win, but we just don't have time to devote to help you achieve your goal." One thing that did keep me going is that I met some great people on my way. I met people that were deeply hurting. I met people dealing with cancer. I had the privilege to spend time praying for some of these dear people. This did energize me a bit to keep going. Dear reader, if you want to win over someone's heart don't be a friend that just prays. Be a friend that goes into the battle with them. Be side by side in their fight! Then you will have a friend for life. Remember to invest in the only thing that is eternal in this lifetime, which are relationships. Nothing else goes with you when you leave this life!

The time to turn all of my signatures into the recorder's office was drawing near. This had to be done in the first part of July, so that they could verify all of the signatures before the August 24th vote took place. I made a big push for signatures at the end of June. I even went out on Sundays. This made some people even angrier at me. I couldn't really blame them, but somehow I needed to get on the ballot. When I had finished, I ended up with 1,486 signatures, and I knew at least 1,290 of those were valid. In the first week of July, I took all of my petitions to the County Recorder's Office to be notarized. The signatures had to be counted in my presence by two different county employees. Each of the employees made a tape on the calculator, and they had to make sure the tapes matched each other. One of the employee's tapes didn't match the count, so they had to start all over again. The process of counting took a little over an hour. I signed paperwork that stipulated I agreed to their count. Then I had to wait to see if the opponent was going to challenge me. But I was confident I had enough good signatures, because I had checked them all against the register of voter database. As it turned out, my opponent didn't challenge my signatures. Once that happened, I knew I would see my name on the ballot for constable. I felt all of my hard work was paying off. I had prayed over and over again that if it was God's will for me to be constable that he would allow me to get on the ballot. Since I was on the ballot, I took this as a sign from God that he was behind me in this endeavor.

Now that the signatures were turned in, I still had to get my name out there. I turned back to the data base of voters that I had to help me. This data base allowed me to create a call list. I could establish the parameters of this call list. I knew that I couldn't call all 55,000 registered Republican voters by myself, so I had to come up with a plan. What I ended up doing is choosing to call all of the voters who had voted 4 out of the last 4 elections as absentee voters. Most of these voters were older in age. They were die hard voters having voted the past 4 times in a row. I knew that these people were guaranteed to vote this time around. I needed to spend my time talking to as many of the voters that were going to vote as possible. I spent about 2 hours a day calling through my lists of people. I was able to call over 1,000 people in just a month and a half. A lot of these people on the phone were rude to me as well. How many phone calls do you get during election time at your house? If you're like me, you probably get 10 a day, and they're usually just bashing their opponent. People were getting plain tired of politicians badgering them. I would say, "Hey, at least I'm not a recorded message. I'm the real person calling you." That helped a little. Never once in my campaign did I ever say anything negative about my opponent!

The election took place on August 23rd. I did not sleep well the night before the election. I was a nervous wreck, knowing that either all my work was going to pay off, or I would still be unemployed. My parents came into town to be here for the vote. Finally the day of the vote had arrived. First thing that morning, I got my suit and tie on and went to go vote for myself. It was a weird feeling to see myself on the ballot, and vote for myself. I actually had to look at my name a couple of times, and make sure I was marking myself. My Dad came with me, because I wanted a picture of me inside the polling place, casting my vote. Unfortunately, I was told that was against the rules, and wouldn't allow the photo to happen. Not being able to snap a picture of that important moment made me frustrated! The rest of the day I couldn't sit still for long. I don't believe I had any finger nails left. I could hardly wait for the counts to come in. I was told that the first counts that came in would be from the absentee ballots that had been sent in. Those numbers would come in around 8p.m. Since I was a candidate, I was invited to be at the Convention Center in Phoenix, AZ to watch the votes as they came in. My parents were kind enough to watch our kids while Laura and I went to this event.

We arrived at the Phoenix Convention Center around 7 p.m. I thought this place would have been packed, but there were very few people in attendance. I saw three news crews set up just in case a big political candidate were to show up. Most of the big candidates had enough money to book a private room to watch the results and celebrate in with their family and friends. In the front of the main room there were four huge screens. On those screens they had

175

the voting totals as they would come in. I could hardly wait until 8 p.m. for the first votes. My wife was trying to calm me down by holding my hand. I was a complete nervous basket case. Right at 8 p.m., the first votes came across the screen. The names scrolled from top to bottom, so I had to wait about a minute until my race came up. Whichever candidate had the lead would be highlighted in white. When my race came up, I saw my name was highlighted in white, and looked over in amazement at the totals. I had 4,300 votes to my opponent's 4,100 votes. Right out of the gate I had a 200 vote lead. I was jubilant, excited, and in disbelief. Really not knowing how many people overall would eventually vote, I thought the lead was a good one. My opponent was not there that night. However, there were other constables there. Some of them told me that they were shocked to see how many votes I got. It should have been a run away for the opponent. They also said that a 200 vote lead is good, and they offered to help me out when I was elected into office. I was feeling really good. I said "Thank you Jesus," several times! I was excited that after 20 years of going after my dream job, it was finally here. I was, for all intents and purposes, counting my chickens before they had hatched.

At about 9 p.m., the votes from the polls started to come in. When the first numbers were put up I had lost some of my lead, but was still ahead by 190 votes. About every 20 minutes the numbers were updated. It was pins and needles for me all night. The next numbers came up, and I had a 175 vote lead. Then the next time I had a 160 vote lead. My lead was slowly vanishing. By midnight that night, I had a 9 vote lead. The newspaper the next day showed me as a winner in the race. That's a keepsake item that I laugh at often! Now the grueling wait was upon me, because the people who didn't send in their absentee ballots on time were allowed to drop them off at the polling place on election day, but they weren't all counted for about a week. Do you think I slept very well this whole week? Why do I put myself through such torture in life? By the next day, I was down 20 votes. I had heard that there were thousands of ballots still to count. I kept saying that even if I get 51% of those votes, it can turn around for me. The next day I was down 60 votes. The third day after I was down 210 votes. This day pretty much put the nail in the coffin. When the election results were made final, it was about 8,174 votes for me, and 8,479 votes for my opponent. I "Almost" won the election to become a constable. I missed it by 305 votes.

Philippians 3:12- 4:1 says, "Not that I have already obtained all this, or have already been made perfect, but I press on to take hold of that for which Christ Jesus took hold of me. Brothers, I do not consider myself yet to have taken hold of it. But one thing I do: Forgetting what is behind and straining toward what is ahead, I press on toward the goal to win the prize for which God has called me heavenward in Christ Jesus. All of us who are mature should take such a view of things. And if on some point you think differently, that too God will make clear to you. Only let us live up to what we have already attained. Join with others in following my example, brothers, and take note of those who live according to the pattern we gave you. For, as I have often told you before and now say again even with tears, many live as enemies of the cross of Christ. Their destiny is destruction, their god is their stomach, and their glory is in their shame. Their mind is on early things. But our citizenship is in heaven. And we eagerly await a Savior from there, the Lord Jesus Christ, who, by the power that enables him to bring everything under control, will transform our lowly bodies so that they will be like his glorious body. Therefore, my brothers, you whom I love and long for, my joy and crown, that is how you should stand firm in the Lord, dear friends!"

I must realize that I'm but an alien in this world. I am being taught that no matter what the outcome is, I must affix my eyes on the true prize. I don't believe God wants us to give up on our hopes and dreams. But he does want us to understand that those hopes and dreams shouldn't define who we are. If we let the world define us, it will bring us to ruin. Stand firm, and know whatever the outcome is that Christ has a better view of the bigger picture then you or I do. After all, my rewards in heaven someday will far outweigh any win accomplished on earth!

Chapter 8 "Almost" gave up on God.

Dear reader if you're anything like me, you have had moments in life where you "Almost" gave up on God. There's a big wide range that the "Almost" giving up on God fits into. It could mean that you shook your fist at God in anger, asking why something happened, or didn't happen. It could mean that you doubt the power of God in your life like Peter did in Matthew 14:28-31, where it says "Lord, if it's you," Peter replied, "tell me to come to you on the water." "Come," he said. Then Peter got down out of the boat and walked on the water to Jesus. But when he saw the wind, he was afraid and beginning to sink, cried out, "Lord, save me!" Immediately Jesus reached out his hand and caught him. "You of little faith," he said, "why did you doubt?" To the other extreme, you end up turning 180 degrees, and walk the other way from God. I believe as Christians our "Almost" giving up on God starts when we take our eyes off of Jesus. At that time we immediately begin to sink. Jesus always has his hand outstretched to keep us from completely sinking.

In this chapter I'm going to go into more detail about the moments in my life that I "Almost" gave up on God. Some of those moments I have briefly told you about in the prior chapters of this book. What I didn't do is go in depth about my deep feelings at those times. I believe it's important that you know even people that believe in Christ have deep struggles. Any Christian that would tell you that they have never had an "Almost" give up on God moment in my opinion is wearing a mask. Even pastors of churches struggle with "Almost" giving up on God. Unfortunately, most pastors believe that if they shared these moments with the church, they would be condemned for it. My prayer is that by me being very open with you, you will be challenged to be open with others as well. Remember it's not the well people that need a doctor, but the sick. A church should be nothing more than a hospital for sinners. But if we're unable to let others know what is ailing us, we ourselves can never be healed. Wearing a mask inside church doesn't keep you from getting sick - it means you're already infected by the lies of this world. As you read through this chapter, please take time to reflect on your life. What were your "Almost" give up on God moments? How did you turn those "Almost" moments around to glorify God? If you're ready, let me dive into this chapter, and pour out my soul to you.

As a Christian, there are several scriptures that I have a tough time swallowing. Especially when I'm in my "Almost" give up on God attitude. I will share some of these verses throughout this chapter, but the first one is Romans 8:28, which says, "And we know that in all things God works for the good of those who love him, who have been called according to his purpose." The other which is similar is Jeremiah 29:11, which says, "For I know the plans I have for you," declares the Lord," plans to prosper you and not harm you, plans to give you hope and a future." Has anyone ever brought those scriptures to your attention when the going is tough? When you're in an "Almost" give up on God moment, are you truly believing that all things that are happening at that time are good for you? I ask, "Really God? This is your plan to prosper me? This is your idea of not harming me? Where's my hope and future in this?" Or in the case of my wife with terminal cancer, where is her hope, and future? I want to give some advice from experience. If you know someone that is going through a rough moment, don't quote these scriptures to them. It will only make them angrier. These are great scriptures with great truth, but not right for all situations. It's like when my Dad would say right before spanking me, "This is going to hurt you more than it hurts me." It's true in a deeper sense, but when you're getting hit it's just not something you need to hear. Instead, let me encourage you to just listen to the other person's tough time. Be a sounding board. Love on them at that moment. Here's me being honest with you. Sometimes the scriptures I would read would cause me to have more doubt then faith that everything would be alright!

The "Almost" giving up on God moments start at an early age. That sin nature in all of us makes us question God's hand in our lives. When I was in elementary school getting beat up "Almost" every day, I would ask God "why?" Now the real reason why I was getting beat up is because I couldn't keep my mouth shut. I was tattling on other kids whenever they were doing something wrong. However, in my mind I wasn't doing anything wrong, because I would say to myself that God wouldn't want these kids to being doing that. I was conflicted with how to take the Jesus I knew, and live that out in a corrupt world. It was as if I demanded that in every situation throughout the day, kids around me had to live for Jesus. If they refused to follow the correct way of doing things, then I felt it was my job to fix it. Looking at it from my point of view today, there's a little paradox to it. The Bible says that unless we have the faith of a child, we can't come to him. Well if we all had the faith of a child, wouldn't we all be more confrontational when it came to our corrupt world? Shouldn't we still have a passion for righting the wrong? The longer I live, the more I think the world is beating the kid out of us. Then we become more like the world, because being beat up all the time really hurts! I often wonder if I would have been a tattle tale or been beaten up if I hadn't grown up in a Christian household? Even though I've pondered that, I'm still thankful to have grown up in a loving Christian home.

When I was just twelve years of age, I experienced another "Almost" gave up on God moment. If you remember, I was still not popular at all. I noticed that all of the kids that seemed popular wore glasses. Every night I would pray that I would have to wear glasses. Well as you saw in chapter one, I finally had to get glasses for reading. I had to wait two weeks for my glasses to arrive. This was before they had a one hour eyeglass place. I remember being very excited when my glasses came in. The first day I walked into class with my glasses, I was so happy. After all, I prayed to God to get glasses, so I could be popular. God answered my prayer, so I knew it would work. As my chest puffed out, I pulled out my glasses from their brown case. I slowly put them on. I purposely looked around to all of the kids in my class to make eye contact with them. I intentionally wanted them to see me with my glasses on. Well, right away I was made fun of. I was even being made fun of by the kids in my class that already wore glasses! That certainly never made much sense. I was called "four eyes". I had never felt as ugly as I did that day. It wasn't solely because the kids were making fun of me. I remembered thinking "God why would you answer my prayer allowing my eyesight to get poorer, if in the end it wouldn't help with my popularity?" It seemed so irrational to me at the time. God intentionally hurt me only to hurt me more! I said, "God if it wasn't going to help me be more popular, then wouldn't it have been better to just leave my eyesight the way it was?" I started to believe that maybe God doesn't exist, and it was just a coincidence that my eyes got bad. I didn't want to believe God would hurt me. I felt this was a curse that I now had to live with the rest of my life. I wore reading glasses all the way until I turned 39, when I had to get bifocals. This was truly an "Almost" give up on God moment. You may ask how such a small thing such as wearing or not wearing glasses could become such a moment. Well, it made me doubt God! Whenever something makes us doubt God's path for our lives, it falls into the category of "Almost" giving up on God. When you're young it's hard to truly reflect adequately on these moments. Years later, I did reflect on this whole eyeglasses ordeal. I believe God was telling me, "Dale, your life is out of focus right now. You're asking me for diminished eyesight, so you can be popular." God was saying, "Dale, most children pray at night that they can have their eyesight restored, and you intentionally want poorer vision?" God has a sense of humor sometimes to get his point across to us. My eyesight was poor before my eyes were poor! Let me explain. My outlook on life was revolving around what would make me happy. If we see just ourselves and not God, we already have poor eyesight. Our eyes and our focus need to be on God first. God allowed me to get glasses, so I could see him more clearly in the future!

Between the ages of 14 and 15 was a tumultuous time for me. Back when I was growing up, they really didn't have a diagnosis for ADHD, which stands for Attention Deficit

Hyper Activity Disorder. When I would act out, I was just viewed as a rambunctious boy. Well when you throw ADHD and puberty in the mix together, the combination is not good. I was at the age where I was trying to desperately find my identity. What was my purpose in life? Why was I here on earth? I still had no friends at school, or in my church youth group. I imagine my ADHD had to account for a lot of my problems socially. People in general pull back from people that are very outgoing. I wanted so desperately to talk to someone about all of the stuff in life that was getting me down. The more I seemed to reach out to others, the more I was shunned. For some reason, I just felt that my parents wouldn't understand. When you're young it feels that your parents are out of touch, when in fact they most likely went through similar feelings themselves. The more depressed I got, the easier it was for me to become agitated. It didn't take much to cause me to lose my temper. On one occasion, I even put my fist through the bathroom door. I didn't want to be out of control, but I just didn't know how to be in control. Even though I was going to church every week, I didn't feel that God cared about what I was going through. I thought that if God cared, then why are other Christian kids shunning me? Shouldn't these kids from church at least like me? I was close to giving up on myself. I figured the only way to stop the pain inside me was to take my own life. This would have been the ultimate way of giving up on God, if I had went through with it. The only reason I didn't take my life, was because a pastor had once said that if I did, that I would end up in Hell. I felt like I was in Hell already, and wasn't enamored by the idea of spending an eternity in there. So in the end, I only "Almost" gave up on God.

At the age of 19, I was engaged to be married to Laura. We were living together without the benefit of marriage. At that time, I was planning on spending the rest of my life with Laura, so I didn't think it was a big deal to live together. The church had another idea totally. As I described in a prior chapter the senior pastor enacted tough love on the both of us. He told us to either get married, or stop living together. If I choose neither, I wasn't welcome to attend his church. My thoughts at that time were, "You have to be kidding me! I have been in this church since I was a week old. This pastor hasn't been here as long as I have. What right does he have to treat me like this? Isn't church all about love and acceptance? What about tolerance for others?" I felt that if the church was kicking me out, then God didn't really exist. It felt as if I was living a lie all these years. Surely there were other church members with sin in their lives. Why was I being singled out? I ended up walking out on God and church completely, until I got married. That was a dark 5 year period in my life. I was backsliding and doing things the way Dale wanted to do them. How could this pastor know that his tough love would eventually work? I don't think he could, but he had to trust God to work out all of the particulars in my life. I'm going to interject an opinion. Our churches are too worried about attendance numbers, and what others will think of them if they exhibit tough love. We say we trust in God's plan, but do we really, if we can't exhibit tough love? It took me to "Almost" give up on God in this ordeal to later have a stronger relationship with my Savior!

Even though I was kicked out of the church and was angry

185

at God, I would still find myself blaming Him for things in life. Isn't it amazing that even when someone is not trusting completely in God, they would have the audacity to still blame God? When I was 21 yrs old, and let go from the Mesa Police Department, I shook my fist at God. Why would you have me move from CA to AZ? It didn't seem rational to me. At 23 yrs old, when I was let go from being a reserve police officer, I was devastated. I wept for weeks after losing this position. I literally banged my fists and head against my bed. I slept the days away. I reasoned that I couldn't hurt when I was asleep, and time would go by much faster that way. I constantly told Laura that God didn't love me. When I lost the election, I was still searching for answers. Quick note: If your mind isn't right, then looking in the bible for the answer can make things worse. For instance, I came across these verses in Romans 9:20-21. They say, "But who are you, O man, to talk back to God? Shall what is formed say to him who formed it, 'Why did you make me like this?' Does not the potter have the right to make out of the same lump of clay some pottery for noble purposes and some for common use?" This was a very tough verse for me to swallow. To be honest, I still wrestle with this verse on occasion. We can't argue with the creator about how we were made. God has the right to choose which creations will be noble, and which will be for common purposes. What a dagger in my heart. I thought I had solved the mystery when I came across these verses. For whatever reason, God chose to make me out of the clay used for common purposes. I was convinced of it. I looked back over my last 23 years, and I had nothing remotely positive to show for it. This verse "Almost" caused me to not only give up on God, but to not even read the bible anymore. If I was just common material then I would live out my life as a commoner away from God. I came to realize much later that by keeping me a commoner, God was in fact preparing me for noble purposes later in life. For instance, if I didn't have all of these common experiences, there would have been no need to write this book. I felt the Lord convicting me to write this all down to make sure you know that your common moments or "Almost" moments can be used for God's noble purpose.

When I was 24 years old I got married. I was welcomed back into the church after that. I started to once again go to church each Sunday. Even though I felt closer to God then I had for the previous 5 years, I was still using God for my own purpose instead of letting God use me for his purpose! After being let go as a reserve police officer, I had a little over 2 years left before my certificate from the academy would expire. If you have ever gone through the process of trying to get a job in law enforcement, you will understand the agony I faced. Each application process can take anywhere from 3-7 months on average from start to finish. Usually I started by filling out a huge application packet. Then I waited. If my application was accepted, I would usually get a letter letting me know when the next written test would be held. When I would show up for the written test, there would usually be 100-200 other applicants there taking the test as well. The department would say that they were looking to fill 3-5 positions. The odds of being hired were made pretty obvious, If the written test was passed, I'd get a call back to do the physical agility test next. Most departments had a standardized test in this area. Depending on a person's age, there were different requirements. For me I had to do 35 push-ups, and 52 sit-ups in a minute.

Then I had to be able to run 1.5 miles in under 12 minutes, 51 seconds. This wasn't hard for me to complete, it was just tedious to do it so many times. After that, if the agency was still interested, they would call me back for an oral interview. Usually there are at least 3 people on the panel. The interview is generally an hour long. If they were still interested after the panel interview, a back ground investigation was begun. After that, they set up a polygraph test. That in itself is interesting. A lot of weird questions are thrown at you. I was told by some of the polygraphers after going through all of the drug questions (and you would be surprised how many different drugs are out there) that I was somehow beating the machine. They would tell me that there's no way in the world that I didn't try one of the drugs they listed. Their non-belief made me sad. I was thinking that must mean the majority of people they hire had tried drugs at some point. I was actually told on more than one occasion that I didn't have enough life experience because I hadn't taken drugs! On one test, the administrator asked me if I had ever stolen anything. He said, "You're lying, the test is over." I said, "Why, I haven't stolen anything?" He asked me what I was thinking about. I said that my mother had made cookies for church, and for me not to take any of them. He laughed, and gave me the benefit of the doubt. Then he started the test again and asked, "Other than stealing cookies from your mother, have you stolen anything?" I responded "No". He said there was no way I was telling the truth. This was an agency that thought I was too naïve, so I wasn't hired. If you make it through the 3-4 hour polygraph, they will set you up with a physical that is unlike any normal physical that you have ever had. Just imagine this process done over, and over again. I explained this process so you can get a better idea of why I was so frustrated.

I literally gave myself writer's cramps filling out applications. I felt pressured to get hired onto an agency before my certificate expired. I spent over $26,000 to put myself through the academy. I figured there would be some agency that would want to save themselves money by hiring me, since they wouldn't have to put me through another academy. I was working various armed security jobs to try to demonstrate to law enforcement agencies that I was still serious about pursuing a career as a police officer. Before my certificate expired, I estimate that I had put in applications for over 425 police agencies. No one could say that I didn't get hired for lack of effort! During this process I got really close a few times to getting hired. I would get my hopes up whenever the agency would send a background investigator to talk with people I knew, since that happens at the very end of the hiring process. But each time, I was let down. When those rejections came, I was right back to blaming God for the hurt He was allowing me to face. I was not always nice to my wife, either. God granted her such an extra measure of patience with me. I'm not sure I could take it if the roles were reversed. As the date approached when my certificate would expire, and all my work was thrown down the drain, I really doubted God's work in all of it. I was depressed with the life I chose, and the mistakes I had made. I constantly blamed myself. I looked at other's that were getting into law enforcement, and would tell myself I'm more qualified than they are. I saw firsthand the unequal hiring standards that took place. I was having another moment where I "Almost" gave up on God. In Matthew 5:45 it says, "He causes his sun to rise on the evil and the good, and sends rain on the righteous and the unrighteous. Let me ask you a question. Have you ever felt that it's raining on the righteous more than it's raining on the unrighteous? Still today the only way I can wrap my brain around this verse is thinking of it this way. I believe that it only appears that the unrighteous are not getting rained on, because they look successful. But are they really happy? Being separated from God means they constantly have a dark cloud following them. The unrighteous are just better at wearing a happy mask, but if they were truly honest, they would show their pain. I learned that I really needed to focus on my relationship with God, and let him worry about all of the other unfair stuff. This is no small feat. I still struggle every once in awhile with this today.

I was 31 yrs old when my wife was diagnosed with terminal cancer. When my wife was diagnosed with cancer, it meant that I had a form of the disease as well. I already took you through a lot of this journey in chapter 4 pretty thoroughly. This has been the biggest trial of my life, so I will highlight the areas where I "Almost" gave up on God during this time. Right off the bat when the neurosurgeon introduced us to hospice, I said "Why, God?. My wife is only 30 yrs old! She has never drunk, smoked or done anything unhealthy to deserve this." In moments of such heartache, I believe we all question God. I shook my fist at God after the diagnosis. The surgeon gave my wife a 50/50 chance to survive brain surgery. The whole week before the date of the surgery I was questioning God's existence. Surely a loving God wouldn't put us through all of this. On the flip side, when she made it through her surgery, I was giving praise to God. Oh how fickle we humans can be. God is great if things are going well, and not great when they're not. God needs to be great in our eyes all the time. About a week after the surgery, my wife had twenty blood clots in her lungs. When I was told my wife wouldn't live through the night, I was livid with God. Again, I was back to questioning why I spent time reading the Bible or praying when it all came down to this. Not only did I "Almost" give up on God, but I "Almost" gave up on being married. I was sure that my wife was going to pass away soon. I was on the phone with a female friend that very night wanting someone to hold me, should my wife die. I didn't want to be alone. My world was crashing in around me.

Because of the blood clots in my wife's lungs, she would have to go on blood thinners for the rest of her life. About one year after this incident, we were traveling on the freeway, and traffic started to stop in all 5 lanes. I was in the fast lane at the time. I looked up in my rear view mirror, and saw a minivan coming up very fast. Traffic was already stopped ahead of me, and to the side of me. There was nowhere for me to go. I said "Hold on," and then a loud crash. We were hit in the rear at about 60mph by a person that didn't have a license, or insurance. My wife said she couldn't feel her legs. The first thought going through my mind was that she was internally bleeding due to the blood thinners. If she was internally bleeding, she was going to die right there in front of me and our two young kids. My oldest was about 5 years old and my youngest 1 year old. They were both in the back seat screaming, and scared. When the fire department got there they had to use the jaws of life to excavate my wife from the car. I was in the car yelling at God again. "God, why do you keep putting my wife in harm's way? God it isn't fair! This other person shouldn't even be driving a car! Why couldn't she hit someone else?" I said, "God, we just finished Laura's treatments. It's been a really hard year. We were just starting to get back some normalcy in our lives. Why, God, did you bring more calamities on us? Where were you right before the accident? Were you sleeping on the job? Where were your angels? Where is your hand of protection on our lives?" I was slamming my closed fist against the steering wheel the whole time. I was just plain ticked off at everything. I was at my wits end, and didn't think I could handle anymore adversity. I "Almost" gave up on God that night.

There were so many up and down moments through my wife's illness, that I can't possibly record every moment that I "Almost" gave up on God. To be honest with you, I'm a bit ashamed to say that there were a lot of moments that I questioned God during this time. When my wife came out of remission, and had to do a second round of radiation, I was mad at God again. When she had to go back on chemo again, I was mad! It's just so emotionally draining day in and day out, living with a person with cancer. I understood why statistics don't favor couples staying married through this awful disease. I had to take over a lot of the chores around the house. That meant working a full time job, and coming home to work some more. I wasn't able to count on my wife feeling good enough to get things done. And I knew that intimacy was the furthest thing from my wife's mind. Cancer will push a family to the brink of insanity. Even though I shook my fist at God, I know deep down that if I didn't have my faith in God, I wouldn't be able to continue this journey.

About a year and a half ago, my wife had another major setback with her brain cancer. She was unable to speak for three weeks. I had always taken for granted hearing my wife's voice. For the first seven days of this three week period, she couldn't communicate at all. Then she was able to write some things down on paper, but a lot of it didn't make much sense. My two kids at the time were 12 and 8 years old. For them not to hear their mom's voice was devastating to them. My boys would constantly ask if their mom was going to die. It was hard to put them to bed at night. They would stay up crying most of the night. They wanted to not only tell their mom that they loved her, but also to hear her say "I love you," back to them. What a trying time this was for the entire family. I thought for sure that I was going through the final weeks, or months of my wife's life. I was crying out to God again to heal my wife, and let her speak again. In the same breath, though, I was having a lot of moments where I "Almost" gave up on God again.

After reading an MRI scan of my wife's brain, the neurologist told us she wasn't sure if her speech would come back, or not. She said that the cancer had come out of remission, and was now a stage 4 tumor. This is the worst, most aggressive form of brain cancer at this point. Again, the doctors thought that my wife would have months left to live. When she finally started communicating with us again, we started to have hope. The neurologist said she knew of a radiologist that would give her a second round of radiation. Laura agreed to sign her life away to go through another round of radiation. She has now been given an amount of radiation equal to two lifetimes. The doctors really weren't sure if there would be any affect on the tumors. Well, the four tumors shrunk in size. We were told that this would buy her more time. She went back on chemo again. Then most recently, the doctor saw some more small growth. The decision was made to give her IV chemo along with the oral chemo she was already on. The doctor stated that she will now be on chemo the rest of her life.

When someone is told they won't ever be able to stop taking poison for the rest of their life, it feels like a death sentence for sure. My wife has lost a lot of weight during this double chemo. I again would go back to God praying for healing. "God, please take this chemo away. Please remove the tumors from her brain." But as time goes by, I have doubts that God will do another miracle like he did in the past. I feel that it's already been a miracle that she has lived as long as she has. How much more time will God give us with Laura? I have asked God to either heal her, or just take her home. This is a selfish prayer, but I literally get mentally exhausted. I'm constantly wondering what will be the last word I hear my wife say to me. What will be the last word I say to her? Lately, her right leg has started to get weak. She now has to have a walker to get around. I'm yelling at God again, "Hasn't my wife, and family been through enough? How much hurt are you going to make us all endure?" If you have ever had someone close to you with a terminal illness, I'm sure you can relate to me. Our human nature is to pray for healing, and if we don't see the healing when we expect it, then we go back to blaming God again. To be honest I can't tell you that I won't have a lot more moments where I

"Almost" give up on God through this process. I do pray that it will always be just "Almost" even through all of the pain that I'm certain is ahead of me. I try to hold onto the fact that God's healing is sometimes manifested in taking the person home to heaven where a perfect body is awaiting. This is the ultimate form of healing for us all. This is what as Christians we long for. So why do I still shake my fist at God? I want life to be fair. I want my wife to live long enough to see her kids grow up, and get married. I want my wife to be a grandmother someday. I want for her a long life that is promised in the Bible for those who follow Christ. If we get anything short of a long life, then I feel like we've all been cheated! For now me, and my family are still on the emotional roller coaster. Dear reader, I ask that you include me and my family in your prayers.

A year ago, I was working as a General Sales Manager for a telemarketing company. It was a horrible job to have to wake up and go to each day. A majority of the workers were previously in prison. Drinking and drugs were commonplace. The language at this job was vial. I really didn't know why God wanted me to be at such a place. This job really stretched my faith. But even though it was a horrible place to work it, was still a job, and I did have the opportunity to share my faith with several workers. I pray that God had me there to reach one, or more of these people. I sincerely hope that when I get to heaven someday, I see all of those employees there! The job would have been worth it if even one was reached for Christ. While working there, I had full medical insurance, which is important when you have an ill person to care for. Now the owner of this company was someone I knew even before working with him. I was the manager of his son's little league All Star team Unfortunately, this did not work in my favor, however, as he took issue with how much, and where I played his son on the baseball field. When in actuality, I played everyone's child more than I played my own, so there wouldn't be an appearance of impropriety. I was verbally undressed by him several times. He also sent scathing e-mails, letting me know how much disdain he had for me. For about three months following the ending of the baseball season, the owner ignored me at work. I'm sure he wanted me to quit, but I couldn't, because I needed the job for the benefits. Finally, the owner decided to let me go, stating he couldn't afford me, even though the company was doing better than it had done the previous year. That forced me to go on unemployment, which doesn't pay much. It was a big strain, getting my wife medical care. I was again yelling at God! "I was trying to do my best, Lord. I tried to be a good worker, and a good Christian role model in little league. Why are you allowing this to happen to me? What good will come out of me not having a job? The economy right now is terrible Lord what are you doing?" I was back to shaking my fist at God again. Miraculously, the Lord provided for our every need for the next year. People in church stepped up to help out. Looking back, the Lord was done using me in that awful place. He knew that I wouldn't leave that job on my own, so he forced the issue. He knew I couldn't take much more of that place. God allowed me to be able to take care of my wife and kids during this time. God allowed me to recharge my batteries again. Dear reader, if you lose a job don't fret. When God slams one door closed, he has another door waiting to open for you. It may take more time then you anticipate to open the door. Be patient about

God's timing in opening that door, and in the mean time recharge your batteries!

While being unemployed I had a lot of time to devote to running for the political office of constable. During this process I had so many moments where I "Almost" gave up on God. I will highlight a couple of examples that made me "Almost" give up on God. Growing up in the church, I had always heard how pastors and others would pray for godly leadership for our country. I made the assumption that if pastors wanted godly leadership then they would be willing to back a godly man for a political office. How very wrong I was! Churches don't want anything to do with politics. Again, these were my feelings at this time, please keep that in mind. I felt like saying, "Hey church, if you're not willing to be part of the solution, then keep your mouth shut!" I also thought to myself that the church has become nothing more than a social hangout. Let's go chat with our friends on Sunday, but forget about the rest of the world the other six days a week.

Also during this process, well-intentioned Christians would give me the following verse, and say I will surely win this election: Psalm 37:4 says, "Delight yourself in the Lord and He will give you the desires of your heart." I was told that if I prayed about the election, which I had done numerous times, that God would deliver on this promise. I came to realize later that it's like saying that you can pray to your wallet, and there will be money in it. People like to use prosperity verses, and to be honest, I found myself believing them. You see, I had been on my knees several times asking the Lord to grant me wisdom. I asked the Lord that if this is not where you want your servant to be then don't allow me to get on the ballot. When I made it onto the ballot, how else was I supposed to take it? I took it as a sign that the Lord had answered my prayers, and wanted me to be the next constable. When I felt that the Lord didn't deliver on his promise to give me the desires of my heart, I "Almost" gave up on God again. I would ask other people this theological question: Did the God that created me, and knew me before time began create my innermost desires, or did I create them myself? In other words, this desire to be in law enforcement has been in me from a very young age. Was it God's intent for me to serve him in this field, or did outside factors influence my desires? Most people, including a few pastors, didn't really know the answer. The best answer I got was that it was probably a little of both. God created our desires, and we created our own desires. Well, to this very day it's a hard thing to understand.

Now I love my church, but where were they when I repeatedly asked for help during my election? There was one person willing to get some signatures for me. There were a few others that told their friends that lived in Chandler to vote for me. I did appreciate their efforts for that much. What I really needed was my own church to get behind me. Was giving up even two hours on a Saturday to walk door to door, and get signatures too much to ask? When I was making my phone calls, was it too much to ask that I get someone to make even one hour of phone calls? One hour of calls was equal to about 50 potential voters reached. I felt like my own church was lazy. They said they were praying for me? Did they really expect me to win all on my own? I felt like David must have felt when the Philistine army wouldn't dare go up against the giant

Goliath. They were probably standing behind David saying, "We'll pray for you, but we're not willing to go to battle with you." Like David, all I had to rely on was God. When you don't believe your church is behind you, it makes you want to "Almost" give up on God. So many emotions were running through my head. I talked to my wife and my parents about whether I should look for another church that treated me more like family. The consensus was that I could move to another church, but the people in that new church are still sinners too. They said I would be sorely disappointed again if I believed it would be different in another church. So in the end, I felt if I left my church, I would be doing the very thing I was mad at my own church for not doing, which is standing behind them. How can I be part of the solution if I'm no longer there? I asked God to help me motivate others to take an active role in church.

The night of the election, and the hard week following, really made me "Almost" give up on God. When the first election numbers came up on the screen at 8 p.m., I had a 200 vote lead. Right away I told my wife it was a miracle. The Lord had provided a miracle. The Lord has answered my prayer, and has provided me with a way to have a job that coincides with my desires. As the night went on, my lead slowly slipped. By midnight I had only a 9 vote lead. The whole next week I had to wait for the thousands of absentee ballots to be counted. I didn't sleep very much. It was grueling on my nerves. I'm quite sure I was grating on my own family's nerves. In the end the lead was gone, and I lost by 305 votes. I was very mad at God at this point. Why God would you allow me to go through so much hard work to get on the ballot for nothing? Why God would you allow me to have a 200 vote lead at the beginning, only to take it all away over a week's time? God, if you intended for me to lose, why the lead at the start? God, don't you know that I can't handle this type of stress? Then my mind turned again to, "If I had only made a few more phone calls... If I had only knocked on a few more doors..." Then I thought, "If my own church would have helped me, I surely would have made up this 305 vote deficit!" The mind can play so many tricks when emotions are so high. It was a big "Almost" give up on God moment.

2 Timothy 4: 7-8 is a good way to summarize this chapter: "I have fought the good fight, I have finished the race, I have kept the faith. Now there is in store for me the crown of righteousness, which the Lord, the righteous Judge, will award to me on that day-and not only to me, but also to all who have longed for his appearing." In the end, I had to realize that winning every race in this world isn't what God is concerned about. He is concerned about how we run this race not in what position we come in. Dear reader, I encourage you to run the race in a pure, Christ-like fashion. Don't worry about the awards you didn't obtain. When you hit the finish line in life, all you should care about is that the Lord says to you, "Well done, good and faithful servant." That's the prize you and I need to keep our eyes on! The next time you have an "Almost" give up on God moment, I hope you're able to quickly get your eyes back on Jesus, who is at the end of the race with his arms open wide, just waiting for you to cross the finish line of life!

Conclusion: Don't just "Almost" finish!

I would like to leave you with a couple of my favorite passages to help us all finish this journey well. Luke 9:23-26 says, "Then he said to them all: 'If anyone would come after me, he must deny himself and take up his cross daily and follow me. For whoever wants to save his life will lose it, but whoever loses his life for me will save it. What good is it for a man to gain the whole world, and yet lose or forfeit his very self? If anyone is ashamed of me and my words, the Son of Man will be ashamed of him when he comes in his glory and in the glory of the Father and of the holy angels.'" Powerful verses! In order to deny yourself, you must be humble. You must be willing to accept all of the "Almost" moments in your life. This must be done daily. If you don't do this daily, your "Almost" moments will get a foothold on your life. If your goal in life is to get stuff, then you're on the wrong path. I heard a funny saying a long time ago. It goes something like this: "Have you ever seen a hearse pulling a U-haul?" It's a great word picture saying that you can't take it with you when you go. If that's the case, stop trying to obtain the whole world, for in the process you will lose your very self. Lastly, never be ashamed of your Savior! Stand up for Jesus whenever possible. Always be ready to give a word of testimony about what the Lord is doing in your life! Dear reader, remember that in this life we're all made up of a lot of "Almost" moments. Stay in close proximity to the Lord, so one day he will turn your "Almost" body into a perfect one!

The last passage I would like to leave you with is a prayer by David in 1 Chronicles 29:10-13: "Praise be to you, O

Lord, God of our father Israel, from everlasting to everlasting. Yours, O Lord is the greatness and the power and the glory and the majesty and the splendor, for everything in heaven and earth is yours. Yours, O Lord, is the kingdom: you are exalted as head over all. Wealth and honor come from you; you are the ruler of all things. In your hands are strength and power to exalt and give strength to all. 'Now, our God, we give you thanks, and praise your glorious name."

Dear reader, thank you so very much for taking this journey of "Almost" with me. I pray that you will seek God in all of your "Almost" moments. I look forward to meeting you in Heaven when our lives "Almost" journey's end, and our perfection in Jesus starts. I would love to hear from you. If you were encouraged by this book, it would be an encouragement to get that feedback from you. If you have a prayer request you would like to share, I would love to pray for you. I read all of my own e-mails and respond to each of them myself. I can be reached at dalepresley@cox.net. May the Lord bless you!